Article 20

Children Deprived of Their Family Environment

A Commentary on the United Nations Convention
on the Rights of the Child

Editors

André Alen, Johan Vande Lanotte, Eugeen Verhellen,
Fiona Ang, Eva Berghmans and Mieke Verheyde

Article 20

Children Deprived of
Their Family Environment

By

Nigel Cantwell

International Child Protection Consultant, Geneva

and

Anna Holzscheiter

Assistant Professor, Freie Universität Berlin

MARTINUS
NIJHOFF
PUBLISHERS

LEIDEN • BOSTON
2008

This book is printed on acid-free paper.

A Cataloging-in-Publication record for this book is available from the Library of Congress.

Cite as: N. Cantwell and A. Holzscheiter, "Article 20: Children Deprived of Their Family Environment", in: A. Alen, J. Vande Lanotte, E. Verhellen, F. Ang, E. Berghmans and M. Verheyde (Eds.) *A Commentary on the United Nations Convention on the Rights of the Child* (Martinus Nijhoff Publishers, Leiden, 2008).

ISSN 1574 8626
ISBN 978 90 04 14873 4

CONTENTS

LIST OF ABBREVIATIONS

1986 Declaration	1986 UN Declaration on Social and Legal Principles relating to the Protection and Welfare of Children, with special reference to Foster Placement and Adoption Nationally and Internationally
CCPR	1966 International Covenant on Civil and Political Rights
CESCR	1966 International Covenant on Economic, Social and Cultural Rights
CRC	1989 Convention on the Rights of the Child
ECOSOC	United Nations Economic and Social Council
FAO	Food and Agriculture Organization of the United Nations
GPID	1998 Guiding Principles on Internal Displacement
ICDC	International Child Development Centre (now UNICEF Innocenti Research Centre)
ISS	International Social Service
OAU	Organisation of African Unity
PACE	Parliamentary Assembly of the Council of Europe
UDHR	Universal Declaration of Human Rights
UN	United Nations
UNHCR	United Nations High Commissioner for Refugees
UNICEF	United Nations Children's Fund
WHO	World Health Organization

AUTHOR BIOGRAPHY

Nigel Cantwell (UK) is a consultant on child protection, based in Geneva. He holds an MA in Economics from the University of Cambridge, UK, and a Diploma in Applied Social Studies from Nottingham University, UK. He has been working on children's issues at the international level since the mid-Seventies, first with the now-defunct International Union for Child Welfare, then setting up Defence for Children International during the International Year of the Child, 1979. Throughout the Eighties he was Coordinator of the NGO Group for the Convention on the Rights of the Child, taking part in the drafting of that treaty. He also participated in the development of the UN Rules for Protection of Juveniles Deprived of their Liberty and the 1993 Hague Convention on Intercountry Adoption. In 1994, he began working as a full-time consultant on children's rights with UNICEF, going on to head up the 'Implementation of International Standards' unit at UNICEF's Innocenti Research Centre in Florence, 1998–2003. His main areas of expertise are children without parental care, intercountry adoption issues and juvenile justice. In addition to undertaking advisory and assessment tasks in these spheres, he is currently (2006) involved in particular in the development of UN Guidelines for the protection of children without parental care.

Anna Holzscheiter (Germany) is Assistant Professor at the Centre for Transnational Relations, Foreign and Security Policy, Freie Universität Berlin. She has a background in international relations and communication studies and completed her Master's Degree at the University of Westminster, London, UK. Her doctoral thesis (Freie Universität Berlin) dealt with the 'International Politics of Childhood' and discussed the drafting of the UN Convention on the Rights of the Child from a socio-linguistic perspective, closely following the communicative and social practices that brought about the document. Related to her interest in child protection and children's rights in international politics, she undertook several consultancies for UNICEF in Geneva and Florence between 2003 and 2005. Her research interests are international norm diffusion and children's rights, the global politics of childhood, the collaboration of non-state actors in norm-setting at international level and new modes of governance between public and private actors.

TEXT OF ARTICLE 20

ARTICLE 20

1. A child temporarily or permanently deprived of his or her family environment, or in whose best interests cannot be allowed to remain in that environment, shall be entitled to special protection and assistance provided by the State.

2. States Parties shall in accordance with their national laws ensure alternative care for such a child.

3. Such care could include, inter alia, foster placement, kafala of Islamic law, adoption or, if necessary, placement in suitable institutions for the care of children. When considering solutions, due regard shall be paid to the desirability of continuity in a child's upbringing and to the child's ethnic, religious, cultural and linguistic background.

ARTICLE 20

1. Tout enfant qui est temporairement ou définitivement privé de son milieu familial, ou qui dans son propre intérêt ne peut être laissé dans ce milieu, a droit à une protection et une aide spéciales de l'Etat.

2. Les Etats parties prévoient pour cet enfant une protection de remplacement conforme à leur législation nationale.

3. Cette protection de remplacement peut notamment avoir la forme du placement dans une famille, de la kafala de droit islamique, de l'adoption ou, en cas de nécessité, du placement dans un établissement pour enfants approprié. Dans le choix entre ces solutions, il est dûment tenu compte de la nécessité d'une certaine continuité dans l'éducation de l'enfant, ainsi que de son origine ethnique, religieuse, culturelle et linguistique.

CHAPTER ONE

INTRODUCTION*

1. Article 20 of the UN Convention on the Rights of the Child (CRC) addresses children who are not able to live with their families, either because they have lost or become separated from them for a wide variety of reasons or because a competent authority has determined that it is in the child's best interests to be removed from his or her family environment. At first sight, the scope of Article 20 therefore seems quite clear, since it essentially requires States Parties to provide alternative care for children who live outside their family environment. On closer inspection, however, the determination of who should be the beneficiary of Article 20 is less straightforward. As will become evident throughout this Commentary, the scope of Article 20 in terms of defining this 'family environment' is contested. Generally, the term 'children without parental care' seems to be the most widely used catchphrase for children covered by Article 20.[1] However, it appears that the drafters of the CRC already had a wider group of children in mind than only those living without their *natural* or *biological* parents, and this tendency is also reinforced by the emphasis that the Committee on the Rights of the Child (hereinafter termed the CRC Committee) places on children deprived of a broader family environment.[2] The consequences of this definitional divide, for example when discussing the issue of kinship care or child-headed households, will be a recurrent theme of our Commentary.

2. Article 20 covers a field that is not widely broached in existing international human rights law, and the interpretation of its provisions and

---

* December 2006.

[1] See for example: CRC Committee, *Day of General Discussion on Children Without Parental Care* (UN Doc. CRC/C/153, 2006)(available at http://www.ohchr.org/english/bodies/crc/docs/discussion/recommendations2005.pdf) and UNICEF, *Child Protection Information Sheet: Children Without Parental Care* (New York, UNICEF, 2006).

[2] See the concluding observations of the CRC Committee. These always include a broad section on 'Family environment and alternative care'. As the *Legislative History of the UN Convention on the Rights of the Child* states, the Committee also reformulated the informal heading of Article 20 in 1991, which had, until then, been 'special protection measures for parentless children'. From 1991 onwards the Committee referred to the children addressed by Article 20 as 'children deprived of a family environment'; see UNICEF, *Legislative History of the UN Convention on the Rights of the Child* (Geneva, UNICEF, 1996 (UN-SEC-HR/1996/SER.1/ARTICLE.20)). Interestingly, as noted in footnote 1 *supra*, it nonetheless entitled its 2005 Day of General Discussion 'Children Without Parental Care'.

obligations is consequently at a relatively early stage. Compared to many other issues covered by the CRC, however, concern over the situation of children without parental care has a comparatively long history in international law. At present, renewed international attention is being paid to this particular issue-area, with efforts under way to formulate more precise international guidelines.[3] Yet, a look at the concluding observations of the CRC Committee brings to light an apparent lack of international, regional and national legislative and administrative measures regarding the improvement of the situation of children without parental care:[4] most State reports do not include precise disaggregated data for children living outside their family environment, nor do most States have comprehensive monitoring tools and standards to ensure that alternative care institutions (many of which are provided by private actors) follow the highest standards possible and ensure the best interests of the child.[5] Even in cases where governmental authorities have formulated national guidelines for the protection of children without parental care, such as Tanzania, State reports evidence that these guidelines are not applied consistently.[6] Absence of data, over-institutionalization and over-privatization of alternative care for children deprived of their family environment,[7] the lack of possibilities for children to 'communicate their concerns and complaints regarding their placement in institutions'[8] and the lack of monitoring mechanisms, standards and regulations governing institutions[9] are, thus, the main concerns of the CRC Committee. The frequency with which these issues are cited in its concluding observations demonstrates that infringements of the rights of children deprived of their family environment continue to be widespread.

---

[3] International Social Service/UNICEF, *Improving Protection for Children Without Parental Care. A Call for International Standards*, A Joint Working Paper (New York/Geneva, UNICEF, 2004).

[4] See for example CRC Committee, *Concluding Observations: Mexico* (UN Doc. CRC/C/MEX/CA/3, 2006), para. 37.

[5] All of the CRC Committee's concluding observations contain a section on 'Family environment and alternative care' and most of them voice concern over the situation of children without parental care.

[6] CRC Committee, *Concluding Observations: Republic of Tanzania* (UN Doc. CRC/C/TAN/CO/2, 2006), para. 36.

[7] CRC Committee, *Concluding Observations: Colombia* (UN Doc. CRC/C/COL/CO/3, 2006), para. 55; *Latvia* (UN Doc. CRC/C/LVA/CA/2, 2006), para. 32; *Lebanon* (UN Doc. CRC/C/LBN/CO/3, 2006), para. 43.

[8] CRC Committee, *Concluding Observations: Uzbekistan, Finland* (UN Docs. CRC/C/UZB/CO/2, 2006; CRC/C/15/Add.272, 2005).

[9] See for example CRC Committee, *Concluding Observations: Thailand* (UN Doc. CRC/C/THA/CO/2, 2006), paras. 41–42; *Trinidad Tobago* (UN Doc. CRC/C/TTO/CO/2, 2005), para. 43(c).

3. In 2003, there were an estimated 143 million orphans worldwide, the main causes among many being natural disasters, AIDS and armed conflict.[10] In that sole year, 12 million children in sub-Saharan Africa lost one or both of their parents due to AIDS.[11] Indeed, a 2004 study comparing childhood and childcare patterns across countries in sub-Saharan Africa concluded that no less than one in six households is looking after at least one orphan and that 0.9 percent of these children are double orphans.[12] Over 2 million children in the USA are being raised by a grandparent or other member of the extended family.[13] In 2003, 12,800 unaccompanied and separated children applied for asylum in 28 industrialized countries.[14] UNICEF estimated in 2005 that more than 1 million children in Europe and Central Asia are living in child care institutions.[15] In 2006, the number of internally displaced persons in at least 50 countries ridden by war and conflict was estimated at 23.7 million, the vast majority of these women and children.[16] Together, these numbers provide a graphic indication of the significance of Article 20 on 'children without parental care': at any given time, millions of children around the world find themselves in this situation, temporarily or permanently. Yet, even though these numbers give an overall impression of how far-reaching the scope of Article 20 is and how many children are to be addressed by its provisions, it nevertheless appears that there is an acute 'lack of data and statistics on the number of children without parental care'.[17] And, even in cases where data exist, the indicators used are only rarely comparable across different national contexts, thereby reducing significantly the possibility of making inferences about the broader, 'global' dimensions of children living outside their family environment.[18]

---

[10] UNICEF, *Excluded and Invisible: The State of the World's Children 2006* (New York, UNICEF, 2006), p. 39.

[11] *Ibid.*, p. 16.

[12] R. Monasch and T.J. Boerma, 'Orphanhood and childcare patterns in sub-Saharan Africa: an analysis of national surveys from 40 countries', *AIDS* 18, No. suppl. 1, 2004, pp. 55–65.

[13] U.S. Office of Personnel Management, http://www.opm.gov/Employment_and_Benefits/WorkLife/OfficialDocuments/handbooksguides/Kinshipcare/index.asp, accessed 29 October 2006.

[14] United Nations High Commissioner for Refugees (UNHCR), *Trends in Unaccompanied and Separated Children Seeking Asylum in Industrialized Countries, 2001-2003* (Geneva, UNHCR, 2003), p. 3.

[15] UNICEF Press release, *Children in residential institutions desperately vulnerable to abuse* (Geneva, UNICEF, 31 May 2005).

[16] UNHCR, *Internally Displaced People: Questions & Answers* (Geneva, UNHCR, 2006), p. 4.

[17] CRC Committee, *o.c.* (note 1), p. 10.

[18] For a particularly promising project in this regard see DAPHNE Project Nr. 2002/017/C, *Mapping the number and characteristics of children under three in institutions across Europe at risk of harm*, coordinated by the Centre for Forensic and Family Psychology, University of Birmingham.

4. The wide variety of reasons for which children find themselves living outside their family environment as well as the numerous shapes that 'alternative care' for these children can take, render Article 20 of the CRC a particularly far-reaching obligation for States. Responding to this situation and in particular to a recommendation from the 2005 Day of General Discussion organized by the CRC Committee, several international agencies began formulating a set of proposed guidelines for this specific field of children's rights protection. Apart from these recent activities, however, surprisingly little and only insubstantial international, regional or national legislation has been developed so far to cover the particular situation of children without parental care. Coupled with the broad character of Article 20 (*i.e.* the wide group of children it addresses and the variety of conditions these children might find themselves in), this makes the task of commenting on the article an intricate one. Nonetheless, the imprecision of Article 20 and the relative openness of its provisions leave room for a more general discussion of some of the broader concepts and formulations the article contains and lead us to insist on the need to translate these concepts into clear-cut legal provisions and policies.

5. In this introductory section, certain specificities of this article are addressed – issues that represent the focal point of our Commentary on Article 20: the relevance of the guiding principles of the CRC as formulated by the CRC Committee to this particular article (Title 1.1); the direct obligations this article entails for States Parties to the CRC (Title 1.2); and the CRC's emphasis on the family environment (Title 1.3). In our interpretation of Article 20 and our discussion of complementary human rights legislation in this particular field, we will embrace a broad definition of children deprived of their family environment. Our Commentary will show that international efforts to safeguard the rights of some groups of children falling within the scope of Article 20 – such as unaccompanied minor refugees – are widespread and forceful. In common with efforts in favour of certain other children not in the direct care of their family – notably young detainees – they have, in the past, attracted considerable attention and resulted in a number of international instruments that set out standards which should apply to these children's specific situation.[19] In contrast, other groups of children that we

---

[19] Such as UNHCR, *Refugee Children: Guidelines on Protection and Care* (Geneva, UNHCR, 1994)(Guidelines on Refugee Children) or the UN Rules for the Protection of Juveniles Deprived of their Liberty, adopted by UN General Assembly Resolution 45/113 of 14 December 1990 (Havana Rules).

consider as coming under the definition of children living outside their family environment (*e.g.* homeless and internally displaced children) are largely neglected in international legislation.

1. *Locating Article 20 Within the Wider Framework of the CRC*

6. While of course all of the rights contained in the CRC apply to children without parental care, there are some that have a very special bearing on children who live outside their family environment. When locating Article 20 within the framework of the CRC, one could generally conclude that its broader context is twofold: it can be put in a wider framework by linking it to the so-called 'four P's' contained in the CRC – protection, provision, participation and prevention –[20] and put in a more 'technical' context, *i.e.* related to specific rights contained in the CRC such as, most importantly:

- The child's right to know and be cared for by his or her parents, as far as possible (Article 7(1));
- The child's right not to be separated from his or her parents against their will, except when it is duly determined that this is necessary for the best interests of the child (Article 9(1));
- Recognition that parents or legal guardians have the primary responsibility for the upbringing and development of the child (Article 18(1)) and the requirement that States ensure appropriate assistance to them in this regard (Article 18(2));
- The State's obligation to assist parents and others responsible for the child to fulfil their primary responsibility to secure, within their abilities and financial capacities, the conditions of living necessary for the child's development (Article 27(2)(3)).

7. It is arguable that, in addition to Article 20, the State's responsibility to ensure provision of alternative care is also stipulated elsewhere in the CRC: it is to 'ensure the development of institutions, facilities and services for the care of children' (Article 18(2)), although the intention here, given the context, was surely to focus on day-care.[21] Furthermore, the quality of 'institutions, services and facilities responsible for the care or protection of

---

[20] On the four P's see particularly G. van Bueren, 'Combating Child Poverty – Human Rights Approaches', *Human Rights Quarterly* 21, No. 3, 1999, pp. 680–706 and G. van Bueren (ed.), *International Documents on Children* (Dordrecht, Martinus Nijhoff Publishers, 1993), p. 684.

[21] The *Travaux Préparatoires* do not shed light on the precise intent of this article.

children' is dealt with under Article 3(3) which sets out the State's obligation to ensure that these institutions and facilities 'conform to the standards established by competent authorities, particularly in the areas of safety, health, in the number and suitability of their staff, as well as competent supervision'. Another provision directly linked to alternative care as foreseen under Article 20 is the child's right to the regular review of the necessity and appropriateness of his or her placement for 'care, protection or treatment' and of all other relevant circumstances (Article 25). With regard to longer-term stability in care arrangements for a child, it is also important to note that Article 21 on adoption stipulates that, in cases where 'the child cannot be placed in a foster or an adoptive family or cannot in any suitable manner be cared for in the child's country of origin' (Article 21(b)), consideration may be given to inter-country adoption.

8. Apart from this rather direct interrelation between Article 20 and other articles of the CRC, the relevance of Article 20 to certain general principles of the CRC as defined by the Committee is also noteworthy, particularly to Article 2 that embodies the principle of non-discrimination. In recent years, numerous reports have highlighted the fact that children without parental care face wide-spread discrimination. First of all, discriminatory practices are often responsible for a child's placement in alternative care arrangements, as can be the case, for example, for Aboriginal children,[22] or when children infected with HIV are being 'separated' from their peers and placed in institutional care by official decree[23] or, again, when children with disabilities are routinely placed in institutions.[24] Second, once placed in institutions, these children see themselves confronted with widespread discrimination in terms of access to education, health and other social services. As a consequence, their life opportunities are considerably reduced compared to those of children growing in their family environment.

9. In terms of education, a Chapin Hall study, summarizing experience from Chicago Public Schools, reaches the conclusion that many children in foster

---

[22] See for example: C. Blackstock and J.A. Alderman, 'The State and Aboriginal children in the child welfare system in Canada', *Early Childhood Matters*, No. 105, 2005, pp. 19–22; 'Australian Human Rights & Equal Opportunity Commission', 'Bringing them home (Report of the National Inquiry into the Separation of Aboriginal and Torres Strait Islander Children from Their Families)', Commonwealth of Australia, 1997.

[23] See for instance UNICEF, *Child Protection and Children Affected by AIDS: A Companion Paper to the Framework for the Protection, Care and Support of Orphans and Vulnerable Children Living in a World with HIV and AIDS'* (New York, UNICEF, 2006).

[24] UNICEF Innocenti Research Centre, *Children and Disability in Transition in CEE/CIS and Baltic States* (Florence, UNICEF, 2005).

care face significant academic failure, despite their expectations to graduate from college eventually.[25] In addition, the study found that young people in foster care had much more often repeated grades than their peers living with their natural parents. Similarly, attention has been drawn to the 'dire educational prospects of looked-after children in England'.[26] Certain children without parental care such as children with disabilities, children belonging to minorities or unaccompanied minor refugees might suffer even more widespread discrimination on the basis of their status and, as such, should enjoy particular protection under the Convention and under Article 20.

10. Considering Article 20 in terms of the four central dimensions of the CRC's catalogue of rights, it is evident that safeguarding the rights of children without parental care requires paying attention to all of the so-called 'four P's' of the Convention: participation, protection, provision and prevention. First, States Parties have to assure that the child's best interests are of primary concern in all situations that involve either removal from or loss of family environment, including the child's right to be heard in these proceedings (*participation* dimension).[27] Second, States Parties are directly called upon to provide 'special protection and assistance' to any child deprived of his or her family environment (*provision and protection*). The preventive dimension of Article 20 lies in the circumstance that it is the State's obligation to prevent all those situations that might lead to a child finding him- or herself outside his or her family environment (*e.g.* family break-up, child neglect and abuse, displacement) in the first place. This dimension becomes all the more important when taking into account other key provisions of the CRC, especially obligations to assist families in providing adequate living conditions for their child(ren) (Article 27(3) of the CRC).

11. The primacy of the family established in the CRC and elsewhere makes it the paramount obligation of States Parties to ensure that a child does not

---

[25] M.E. Courtney *et al.*, 'The Educational Status of Foster Children', *Chapin Hall Center for Children Issue Brief*, No. 102, 2004, pp. 1–6.

[26] D. Maxwell, *An Asset Account for Looked After Children; A proposal to improve education outcomes for children in care* (London, Institute for Public Policy Research, 2006).

[27] The participatory dimension is re-affirmed in the Guidelines for Reports by States Parties under the Convention issued by the Committee on the Rights of the Child, where it says that States Parties are requested to provide relevant information on 'how the principles of the "best interests of the child" and "respect for the views of the child" are reflected in their legislative, judicial, administrative or other measures'. See: R. Hodgkin and P. Newell, *Implementation Handbook for the Convention on the Rights of the Child - Fully Revised Edition* (New York, UNICEF, 2002), p. 258.

need an alternative family environment. Should these preventive actions fail, however, States have the responsibility to provide a suitable replacement environment to the child, that prevents further disruption of the child's life ('continuity in a child's upbringing') and takes particular account of the child's cultural needs.

12. The relationship of Article 20 with some of the fundamental principles of the CRC was emphasized in the concluding document of the Day of General Discussion of the CRC Committee in September 2005.[28] Here, the Committee once again underlined the primacy of the family environment, as well as the principle of the best interests of the child that should be ensured more comprehensively in the realization of Article 20. What is more, the final recommendations re-affirm that it is the State's primary responsibility to *prevent* family disruption, family poverty[29] and the potentially resulting breakdown of family structures in the first place and, in case these measures have failed, to provide for alternative family placements for the child without parental care. The variability of the structures and size of these family environments is explicitly and prominently stressed. This seems to suggest that the notion of 'extended family' as enshrined in Article 5 of the CRC should be more systematically taken into account in all actions aimed at ensuring the continuity in a child's upbringing in cases where care by the child's biological parents is not available. The principle of non-discrimination for particularly vulnerable children (such as, most notably, girl children as well as children with disabilities or those infected by HIV) is underlined, and the necessity to respect the child's opinion in all matters concerning alternative family placement is stressed in the Concluding Document of the Day of General Discussion.[30]

2. *Direct Responsibilities of the States Parties*

13. In dealing with the State's obligation to ensure alternative care for children who cannot be looked after by their family, Article 20 broaches what is probably *the* key child protection issue in terms of the unequivocally

---

[28] CRC Committee, *o.c.* (note 1), paras. 6–10, 24–26.
[29] Family poverty is a major reason for relinquishment into care: see as just one example, the State Party report by Estonia, where it is stated that more children are placed in institutions because of economic hardship of their family (27.6 per cent in 1999) than because of 'neglect at home' (UN Doc. CRC/C/8/Add. 45, 2002), para. 197.
[30] CRC Committee, *o.c.* (note 1), paras. 663–664.

direct and comprehensive State responsibility for the well-being of children. In doing so, it also addresses a right that is linked in an unusually direct and intimate manner to many other provisions of the Convention, and its implementation therefore needs to be set not only against the background of the treaty's main thrusts and fundamental spirit but also against a large number of its specific articles. Article 20 applies to a situation where other articles in the Convention addressing the parents', family's or State's obligations *vis-à-vis* the child have already failed to produce a suitable environment for the child's well-being and growing-up. Consequently, State obligations under Article 20 to ensure alternative care for a child take effect not only when it is materially impossible for that child to be cared for by his or her parents – due to death, absence or incapacity – or when it is deemed that the child would be in danger if left in their care, but also because the State has not seen fit or been able to provide, as prescribed in the CRC, adequate and appropriate support to enable the family to remain together.

14. What is more, it can be argued that Article 20 gives expression to the delicate triangular relationship between the child, his or her parents and the State: while other articles are in place to protect family privacy and the rights of parents in guiding and bringing up their child, this article clearly contains the obligation of States to protect the child from a potentially harmful family environment ('cannot be allowed to remain in that environment') and to ensure that there are suitable alternative care options in place that guarantee a minimal disruption of the child's emotional, physical and personal development. However, how these rather general obligations are put into practice by States Parties ('in accordance with their national laws') and what the specific wording of Article 20 implies ('ensure', 'entitled') for the responsibilities of States Parties will be discussed in greater detail in Chapter III of this Commentary ('Scope of Article 20').

3. *The Primacy of the Family Environment*

15. Children living outside their family environment have met with international concern ever since the earliest efforts were undertaken to formulate international principles regarding children's rights. '[T]he orphan and the waif must be sheltered and succoured':[31] among the five brief principles of the 1924 Geneva Declaration on the Rights of the Child, one can already

---

[31] Geneva Declaration on the Rights of the Child, adopted by the League of Nations on 26 September 1924, League of Nations O.J. Spec. Supp. 21, at 43.

make out concern about the situation of children without parental care. Likewise, the vulnerability of children living outside their family environ-ment was addressed in the 1959 Declaration on the Rights of the Child that stipulates in its Article 6: 'Society and the public authorities shall have the duty to extend particular care to children without a family and to those without adequate means of support'.[32] When the first efforts towards a Convention on the Rights of the Child were undertaken some twenty years later, the Polish Government's first proposal, submitted to the UN Commission on Human Rights in 1978, contained an article on children deprived of their natural family environment.[33] Consequently, Article 20 of the CRC relates to a recognized dimension of State obligations on behalf of children in par-ticularly difficult circumstances.

16. In addressing the situation of children 'deprived of their family envi-ronment' (para.1), Article 20 therefore covers, *ex negativo*, one of the most basic tenets of the CRC: the right of the child, as far as possible, to be cared for by his or her parents (Article 7(2)), and this in the context of recogni-tion, in the Preamble, of the family as 'the fundamental group of society'. It thus deals with States Parties' obligations towards all those children that see themselves denied this fundamental right (as expressed in the verb 'deprived of'). As will be discussed in greater detail below, earlier interna-tional treaties already affirmed the primacy of the family as the favourable environment for the upbringing and personal development of a child. Numerous other international treaties have emphasized the perception of the family as the 'fundamental unit of society' (this wording can be found, among others, in the African Charter on the Rights and Welfare of the Child,[34] the CCPR[35] and the CESCR[36]).

17. The family is seen to be the natural environment of the child that ide-ally offers the greatest protection, provision and emotional support to the child – it follows from this that children without parental care must be

---

[32] United Nations Declaration on the Rights of the Child, proclaimed by General Assembly resolution 1386 (XIV) of 20 November 1959.

[33] Article VI of the First Polish Draft contained in 1978 report of the Commission on Human Rights (UN Doc. E/CN.4/1292, 1978).

[34] OAU, *African Charter on the Rights and Welfare of the Child* (OAU Doc. CAB/LEG/24.9/49, 1990), adopted on 11 July 1990, entered into force on 29 November 1999.

[35] International Covenant on Civil and Political Rights (CCPR), adopted by UN General Assembly Resolution 2200A (XXI) of 16 December 1966; entered into force on 23 March 1976.

[36] International Covenant on Economic, Social and Cultural Rights (CESCR), adopted by UN General Assembly Resolution 2200A (XXI) of 16 December 1966, entered into force on 3 January 1976.

considered a particularly vulnerable group of children that requires particular efforts on the part of States Parties. With regard to further specification of situations covered by this article (*e.g.* separation from family by a competent authority, internal displacement, family break-up etc.), there are specific groups of children without parental care whose particular situation is addressed elsewhere in the CRC. Among these groups are: a) children with disabilities (who often grow up in institutionalized care due to their special needs or the inability of their parents to provide adequate support); b) refugee and migrant children; c) juveniles in correctional care and d) children in armed conflict. Others, such as internally displaced children or homeless children, however, are not covered by additional articles in the CRC. In our Commentary, we will specifically discuss the implications of the term 'deprived of' and the variety of situations the term covers, and examine the lack of reference to certain of these situations in the CRC. We will connect this discussion to other fundamental articles of the CRC that address the triangular relationship between parents, the State and the child and, in particular, deliberate upon the wider implications of the concept of the 'extended family and community' as laid down in Article 5 of the CRC. Finally, we will discuss the implications of the fact that Article 20's notion of 'family' covers the family environment, rather than the (biological) parents: we will specifically refer to the bearing this has on alternative care by extended family members and siblings, particularly with regard to increasing recourse to kinship care and the growing number of child-headed households.[37]

4. *Structure of the Commentary*

18. With these initial considerations in mind, the ensuing discussion of Article 20 – its content, scope and the potential problems it raises – mirrors the Article's internal logic that corresponds to the various stages of a child's deprivation of his or her family environment. We will follow the chronology of tracing the process of a child's removal from or loss of his or her

---

[37] Estimates of the numbers of child-headed households are difficult to find – particularly if one is interested in the global scope of this phenomenon. However, numbers given for individual countries already convey how seriously this issue should be taken. In 2001, for instance, the South African Minister of Social Development, Zola Skweyiya, estimated the number of child-headed households in South Africa alone at 248,000; see Opening address to the conference on orphans and other children made vulnerable by HIV and AIDS, available at http://www.sarpn.org.za/documents/d0002100/index.php, published by Southern African Regional Poverty Network.

family environment (stage 1), then move on to the deliberations that lead to his or her placement in alternative care (stage 2) and, finally, discuss the article's relevance for the conditions and standards that have to apply once the child has been placed elsewhere (stage 3). Our review of Article 20 is based on the standards for interpretation laid down in the Vienna Convention on the Law of Treaties:[38] we therefore take into account the *Travaux Préparatoires* of this particular article as well as of other relevant articles of the CRC; the guidelines for reporting set by the CRC Committee; the concluding observations of that Committee; the recommendations made by the Committee after its General Day of Discussion on 'Children without Parental Care';[39] jurisprudence of other international human rights treaty bodies as well as the Human Rights Committee's General Comments No. 16 (right to privacy),[40] 17 (rights of the child)[41] and 19 (the family).[42] We also include, where appropriate, academic literature on children without parental care, particularly on alternative care and, for reasons of illustration and in order to point to certain 'trends' in State practice regarding Article 20, introduce policy initiatives, statistics as well as national and regional case law (most notably from the European Court on Human Rights) where appropriate.

19. Our Commentary revolves around some of the most central concepts contained in Article 20 and attempts to give more 'flesh and bone' to the vagueness in formulation that characterizes certain dimensions of this specific provision – this is done either through internal links with other standards contained in the CRC or by referring to the documentation mentioned above. In particular, we discuss the implications of certain terms contained in this article – terms that implicitly offer further clues as to the scope of this article, especially when seen in conjunction with other central articles and general principles of the CRC. These terms are, more specifically, the expression 'deprived of', the difficulty in defining 'family environment', the

---

[38] Vienna Convention on the Law of Treaties, adopted on 23 May 1969, entered into force on 27 January 1980, http://untreaty.un.org/ilc/texts/instruments/english/conventions/1_1_1969.pdf.

[39] CRC Committee, *o.c.* (note 1).

[40] Human Rights Committee, *General Comment No. 16: The right to respect of privacy, family, home and correspondence, and protection of honour and reputation (Article 17)*, adopted on 8 April 1988.

[41] Human Rights Committee, *General Comment No. 17: Rights of the Child (Article 24)*, adopted on 7 April 1989.

[42] Human Rights Committee, *General Comment No. 19: Protection of the family, the right to marriage and equality of the spouses (Article 23)*, adopted on 27 July 1990.

application of the best interests clause to the situation of children without parental care as well as the implications of the term 'alternative care' along with the qualifiers 'suitable' and 'necessity'.

20. The general argument we develop throughout these discussions focuses on the tension between the requirements to decide on the 'necessity' of alternative placement on the one hand and the 'suitability' of this placement on the other. With regard to the suitability of specific alternative care options, we contend that the implicit 'ranking' that is made in Article 20(3) of the CRC, considering institutional care as inferior to other 'solutions', should be interpreted with precaution: if the term 'institution' is to cover all forms of residential care (by default) then this 'solution' should be considered as no less suitable in certain cases and for certain children, rather than as a second-class solution from the outset. As noted above, children living in institutions in many cases face serious discriminatory practices and considerable limitation in their life opportunities. A 'branding' of institutionalized care as the least favoured environment for children might tend to reinforce these tendencies and contribute to the stigmatization of these children. With regard to the issue of 'necessity', we strongly contend that 'necessity' should be decided on the basis of the child's needs and best interests and not on the basis of what the national system of alternative care is or is not providing.

CHAPTER TWO

COMPARISON WITH RELATED INTERNATIONAL
HUMAN RIGHTS INSTRUMENTS

21. The specific field covered by Article 20 is dealt with in few other international instruments and even then, overall, in very little detail. As a consequence, the interpretation of its provisions and the obligations they imply is at a relatively early stage.[43] Among the few international documents that explicitly address children living outside their family environment is, most notably, the 1986 UN Declaration on Social and Legal Principles relating to the Protection and Welfare of Children (hereinafter 1986 Declaration).[44] Even though, simply as a Declaration with no binding character, it must be considered international 'soft' law, the 1986 Declaration is an important document for two reasons: first, some of its most basic principles and terms have found their way into Article 20 of the CRC and secondly, for many of the issues we will discuss in Chapter III, the 1986 Declaration conveys more substantive meaning to the provisions of Article 20. Apart from the 1986 Declaration, there are various human rights instruments whose scope also covers the specific situation and rights of children without parental care; these will be discussed in the second part of this section, along with certain regional instruments whose references to children living outside their family environment present a pertinent extension and deepening of the standards and obligations of Article 20.

1. *International Human Rights Provisions*

22. Of the major universal or regional general conventions on human rights, none explicitly covers the protection of children living outside their family

---

[43] This will be considerably furthered if and when the initiative, under way at the time of writing (2006), to secure United Nations Guidelines covering the protection of children without parental care comes to fruition, and once the CRC Committee achieves its intention of preparing a General Comment on the issue.

[44] Declaration on Social and Legal Principles relating to the Protection and Welfare of Children, with special reference to Foster Placement and Adoption Nationally and Internationally, adopted by UN General Assembly resolution 41/85 of 3 December 1986 (UN Doc. A/RES/41/85, 1986).

environment. Yet, it is possible to identify certain more general principles – such as the general emphasis on the family as the fundamental unit of society – that are of relevance to Article 20.

1.1   *The 1986 Declaration*

23. *1986 Declaration on Social and Legal Principles relating to the Protection and Welfare of the Child*: Coinciding with the drafting period of the CRC, the UN adopted its Declaration on Social and Legal Principles relating to the Protection and Welfare of the Child in 1986, in which the Member States of the United Nations expressed their concern over the 'large number of children who are abandoned or become orphans owing to violence, internal disturbance, armed conflicts, natural disasters, economic crises or social problems'.[45] This Declaration laid down, for the first time, an international agreement on situations in which 'care by the child's own parents is unavailable or inappropriate'[46] and specified the type and form of alternative care, taking due account of the different ways in which this may be effected, such as the *kafala* of Islamic Law.[47] Some of its more general principles have, therefore, been taken into account during the drafting of the CRC. Although the *Travaux Préparatoires* provide no evidence that the 1986 Declaration directly influenced the wording of Article 20, one can nevertheless conclude that some of its central ideas and formulations have been incorporated into the Convention.

24. Of particular interest to our ensuing discussion in Chapter III is the fact that, in addressing potential forms of alternative care for the child living outside his or her family environment, the 1986 Declaration makes a clear discrimination between care by 'relatives of the child's parents, by another substitute – foster or adoptive – family' on the one hand and, on the other, 'an appropriate institution'. This 'inferred subsidiarity of "institutional care"'[48] results from the formulation 'if necessary' that precedes the term 'appropriate institution'. It is arguable that the particular concern for over-institutionalization of children without parental care that emerged in the course of the 1980s[49] inspired the drafters of the 1986 Declaration to include this qualifier. Subsequently, the restrictive term 'if necessary' found its way

---

[45] Fourth preambular paragraph of the 1986 Declaration.
[46] Article 4 of the 1986 Declaration.
[47] Sixth preambular paragraph of the 1986 Declaration.
[48] International Social Service/UNICEF, *o.c.* (note 3), p. 15.
[49] See for example UNICEF, *Children in Institutions: the beginning of the end? (Innocenti Insight No. 8)* (Florence, UNICEF, 2003).

into Article 20, where this 'ranking' between first- and second-order alternative care options is replicated. We will discuss the implications and potential difficulties resulting from this classification in greater detail in Chapter III below.

25. Despite the overlaps between the 1986 Declaration and Article 20 of the CRC and even though the Declaration's principles do not impose binding legal obligations on States Parties, some of the standards in the 1986 Declaration are stronger than those relating to children without parental care in the CRC. Article 5 of the 1986 Declaration, for example, stipulates that:

> '[i]n all matters relating to the placement of a child outside the care of the child's own parents, the best interests of the child [. . .] should be *the paramount* consideration.'[50] [our emphasis]

26. The applicable best interests clause in the CRC, however, considers the best interests of the child only as 'a primary consideration'. Coupled with the provisions of Article 20, thus, the CRC's interpretation of the child's best interests does not prioritize them. Given the controversies that the *Travaux Préparatoires* reveal on the wording of the best interests clause,[51] the issue of a child's removal can, indeed, be seen as epitomizing a direct conflict between the rights of parents, the rights of the child and the uneasy middle-ground the State occupies with its obligations to protect both the family as well as – in cases covered by Article 20 – the individual child *against* his or her parents or wider family.

27. With regard to the best interests clause, it is also interesting that Article 20 only considers the best interests of the child in terms of the potential removal of the child from his or her family environment (stage 1), while not reaffirming the best interests principle at all with regard to decisions on the alternative placement of the child (stage 2) or regular reviews of the child's situation (stage 3). A further interesting point about the 1986 Declaration is its understanding of 'family'. While Article 20 of the CRC refrains from defining family narrowly as the child's (biological) parents, the 1986 Declaration considers only those children for whom '[. . .] care by

---

[50] Article 5 of the 1986 Declaration.

[51] The 'Legislative History' of final Article 3 of the CRC conveys that there was considerable unanimity among the drafters concerning the issue of whether the child's best interests should be 'a' or 'the' primary consideration in all actions concerning children. Implicitly, this unanimity expressed a friction between those who argued in favour of mitigating children's rights to the benefit of the interests of other parties concerned (the parents), and those who saw the child's best interests as a principle that should precede any other person's or body's interests. See UNICEF, *o.c.* (note 2)(UN-SEC-HR/1996/SER.1/ARTICLE.3).

the child's own parents is unavailable or inappropriate' (Article 4). The 1986 Declaration furthermore posits that '[t]he first priority for a child is to be cared for by his or her parents' (Article 3). A comparison between the two documents leads us to conclude that the 1986 Declaration has a more restricted interpretation of a child's family environment – interpreting family basically as the 'child's own parents' –,[52] whereas Article 20 of the CRC already contains a broader formulation, not making reference to the child's biological parents. The implications of this broadening of social relations and the difficulties attached to this will be discussed further in Chapter III.

28. Generally and not surprisingly, the 1986 Declaration contains more detailed standards than the CRC as concerns the process of a child's removal from his or her family (parents) and alternative placement. In this regard, the Declaration requires, for example, that all those 'responsible for foster placement and adoption procedures should have professional or other appropriate training' (Article 6). Regarding the child's right to be heard and to participate in decision-making that concerns him- or herself directly (as one of the cornerstones of the CRC), it is also interesting that – unlike Article 20 – the 1986 Declaration specifies that 'in all matters of foster family care, the prospective foster parents and, as appropriate the child and his or her own parents should be properly involved' (Article 12). In sum, the 1986 Declaration provides a more far-reaching perspective on the situation of children without parental care, and already applies most central principles later enshrined in the CRC to this particular field of child protection (best interests; participation; primacy of the family), although only explicitly to foster care and adoption.

1.2   The Two 1966 Covenants

29. *The two Covenants*: Even though none of the obligations contained in the CCPR specifically addresses children living outside their family environment, there are various provisions of immediate relevance to Article 20. Article 24, the only child-specific article of the CCPR, provides that the child shall have 'the right to such measures of protection as are required of his status of minor, on the part of his family, society and the State' (para.1). Furthermore, the article stipulates the right of the child to be registered immediately after birth and to have a name and nationality. These rights are of direct importance to Article 20, considering the fact that the iden-

---

[52] Article 5 of the 1986 Declaration.

tity rights of children living outside their family environment – temporarily or permanently – are often in danger (for 'abandoned' or 'relinquished' children and unaccompanied minor refugees, for example) and consequently need strong protection on the part of State authorities and all those concerned with the child's well-being. The CESCR, again, calls for 'special measures of protection and assistance [. . .] on behalf of children and young persons without any discrimination for reasons of parentage and other conditions' (Article 10(3)). The particular vulnerability and dependence of children, thus, is recognized in both Covenants.

30. Both Covenants, as well as the Universal Declaration of Human Rights of 1948, also qualify the status of the family as the 'natural and fundamental group unit of society' (Article 16(3) of the UDHR; Article 23(1) of the CCPR; Article 10(1) of the CESCR) and, with the CESCR stating that the family must be protected and assisted particularly 'while it is responsible for the care and education of dependent children' (Article 10(1)), the Covenants establish that the family is the natural environment for a child's upbringing. Consequently, Article 20 of the CRC reaffirms the superiority of the family environment, be it the 'natural' family environment or an alternative family placement (foster care, adoption) over other types of alternative care, subsumed under the term 'placement in suitable institutions'. The implications of this strong emphasis on the family, as well as the fact that neither Covenant further specifies what is meant by family (*i.e.* the biological parents vs. extended concepts of the family) and that Article 20 also embraces the wider term 'family environment', will be discussed further in the chapter on the scope of Article 20.

2. *Standards Developed for Particular Groups of Children*

31. Apart from general human rights provisions, some of which protect the rights of children without parental care, there are special standards applying to specific groups who can be defined as children 'deprived of their family environment'. Among these, we would emphasize two in particular: the UNHCR Guidelines on Refugee Children and the Interagency Guiding Principles on Unaccompanied and Separated Children.[53]

32. The *UNHCR Guidelines on Refugee Children*, particularly in their Chapter 10 on unaccompanied minor refugees, emphasize the right of the refugee

---

[53] UNHCR, o.c. (Note 19).

child deprived of a family environment to be reunited with his or her family as soon as possible or, in case this is not feasible, to arrange for a substitute family as soon as possible.[54] The Guidelines recognize that unaccompanied refugees are particularly vulnerable and suffer widespread infringements of their fundamental rights such as, for example, the child's right to continuity in upbringing and to a name and nationality. Specific standards are formulated for the reception and treatment of unaccompanied minor refugees concerning, for example, the welfare services they should receive as well as psychosocial and legal counselling and support. Over and above that, the Guidelines contain a definition of an appropriate substitute care environment for unaccompanied minor refugees: 'The most important criterion is that children are provided care that is age-appropriate, loving and nurturing, by continuous care-givers'.[55]

33. The UNHCR Guidelines express particular concern that State practice with regard to status determination of the young refugee often deviates from minimum standards, *e.g.* in terms of recognizing the child's right to be heard, practices as regards age determination, the child's right for legal counselling and appropriate psychological care (especially in case of trauma), the child's right to impartial legal representation by a third person (adult), and the child's right to be adequately and comprehensively informed about all decisions and procedures.[56]

34. The *Interagency Guiding Principles on Unaccompanied and Separated Children*[57] once again confirm most of the basic principles formulated by the UNHCR in its Guidelines and specify four general principles that should be applied to every separated child: the principle of the best interests, non-discrimination, the child's opinion as well as special protection for the girl child. The Guiding Principles require all national and international agencies concerned with unaccompanied and separated children to work towards the

---

[54] UNHCR, *o.c.* (note 19), p. 15.

[55] *Ibid.*, p. 39.

[56] Other international documents addressing the situation of refugee children are UNHCR, *Working with Unaccompanied Children: A Community-Based Approach* (Geneva, UNHCR, 1996); UNHCR, *Guidelines on Policies and Procedures in Dealing with Unaccompanied Children Seeking Asylum* (Geneva, UNHCR, 1997); UNHCR/Save the Children Alliance Brussels, *The Separated Children in Europe Programme: Statement of Good Practice* (Brussels, UNHCR/STC, 2004) and Save the Children UK, *Working with separated children. Field Guide. Training Manual and Training Exercises* (London, Save the Children UK, 1999).

[57] Save the Children/World Vision/UNHCR/UNICEF/International Committee of the Red Cross/International Rescue Committee, *o.c.* (note 53).

preservation of family unity in the first place and, in case where families have been separated, to invest their efforts into family reunification. The Principles' section on 'care arrangements' calls for the child's involvement in all decisions concerning his or her placement in a family or institutional environment, establishes that the child should if possible be provided with a new family within the child's own community, and gives expression to a preference of community care over institutional care 'as [the former] provides continuity in socialization and development'.[58] The Guidelines formulate an extensive catalogue of requirements for a separated child's placement in foster families, calling, *inter alia*, for a regular assessment of the child's situation in the foster family and for assistance for community welfare structures so as to enable fostering within the community. Institutional care is treated with precaution in the Guidelines, which state that 'residential institutions can rarely offer the developmental care and support a child requires and often cannot even provide a reasonable standard of protection'.[59] Finally, the Guiding Principles stipulate that adoption should be considered only in cases where all efforts to trace a separated child's family and to reunite the child with his or her family have failed.

35. Finally here, we would also mention two instruments in the field of juvenile justice: the *UN Standard Minimum Rules for the Administration of Juvenile Justice (known as the 'Beijing Rules')*[60] and the *UN Rules for the Protection of Juveniles Deprived of their Liberty (the 'Havana Rules')*.[61] We do so not because we see juvenile offenders, generally, as being covered by Article 20 – clearly their situation, rights and treatment are dealt with more especially in Articles 37 and 40 of the CRC – but because of the interesting policy parallels these instruments provide. Thus, Article 19(1) of the Beijing Rules stipulates that: 'The placement of a juvenile in an institution shall always be a disposition of last resort and for the minimum necessary period'. This approach is echoed in Article 37 of the CRC and reflects the implied policy thrust of Article 20 in terms of the least possible recourse to institutional placement, stipulating in addition the desirability that institutional care be a temporary, short-term measure. For their part, the Havana Rules set out the conditions under which an institutional placement ordered for a juvenile is to

---

[58] *Ibid.*, p. 43.
[59] *Ibid.*, p. 46.
[60] United Nations Standard Minimum Rules for the Administration of Juvenile Justice, adopted by General Assembly resolution 40/33 of 29 November 1985 (UN Doc. A/RES/40/33, 1985).
[61] *Cf. supra* note 19.

take place and, as we will note in Chapter III, they contain elements of direct interest for interpreting in particular the 'suitability' of residential care placements.

36. Taken together, these standards clearly reaffirm that a) children who are deprived of a family environment are generally considered to be particularly vulnerable to infringements of their basic rights and b) all actions directed towards these children's immediate relief as well as long-term care should conform to the highest standards and be guided by the intent to either reunite the child as quickly as possible with his parents/legal guardians or, in case this is not possible, to provide the child with a stable and harmonious alternative care setting, ideally within a family environment. The documents discussed above also give expression to the general opinion that institutional care should always be considered as a solution of last resort and, as such, corroborate Article 20's emphasis on institutional care as the least desirable solution.

3. Regional Human Rights Instruments

3.1   The African Charter on the Rights and Welfare of the Child

37. The absence of any further international human rights legislation covering the situation of children without parental care is matched by an equal scarcity of instruments at the regional level. The only regional document formulating standards in this regard is the 1990 African Charter on the Rights and Welfare of the Child of the Organisation of African Unity (OAU, now African Union).[62] Articles 18, 19 and 25 of the African Charter address the issue of family dissolution and alternative care in particular. Article 18 generally enshrines the right of the child not to be separated from his or her parents. It provides that a child shall only be separated from his or her parents when a judicial authority determines in accordance with the national law that this is in the best interests of the child. The child deprived of his or her family environment is addressed again in Article 25 on 'separation from parents' – which is, in paragraph 1, aimed at the child 'temporarily or permanently deprived of his family environment, *for any reason*' [our emphasis].[63] The term 'for any reason' already indicates that the OAU's document has a broader set of children in mind, not predominantly those

---

[62] *Cf. supra* note 34.
[63] *Ibid.*

removed from their families, but also those separated from their families for other reasons. This becomes even more obvious in the following paragraphs of Article 25, where it requires States Parties to 'take all necessary measures to trace and reunite children with parents or relatives where separation is caused by internal and external displacement arising from armed conflicts or natural disasters' (Article 25(2)(b)).

38. Interestingly, the African Charter also considers the best interests of the child in the choice of an alternative care solution (see above) in Article 25(3), where it commits States Parties to the following: 'When considering alternative family care of the child and the best *interests of the child* [our emphasis], due regard shall be paid to the desirability of continuity in a child's upbringing and to the child's ethnic, religious or linguistic background'.[64] In this regard, the African Charter is more explicit than the CRC, since it applies the best interests of the child not only to the decision to take the child out of his or her family environment but also to any decision regarding the choice of an alternative placement. It is also noteworthy that the African Charter replaces the term 'solutions' with the expression 'alternative family care of the child' – indicating that a child deprived of his or her original family environment should be placed in alternative family care rather than in some form of institutional care.

3.2   The Council of Europe Recommendation and the European Court of Human Rights[65]

39. Considering the apparent lack of strong human rights legislation with regard to the situation, care and rights of children without parental care, we make reference here to certain developments from the European region that could help, in later sections of this Commentary, to underline some of the most salient issues in the interpretation of Article 20.

40. It is particularly the Recommendation of the Committee of Ministers of the Council of Europe 2005(5)[66] on the rights of children in institutions and

---

[64] *Ibid.*

[65] For a comprehensive discussion of child-specific dimensions of the European Convention on Human Rights see U. Kilkelly, 'The Best of Both Worlds for Children's Rights? Interpreting the European Convention on Human Rights in the Light of the UN Convention on the Rights of the Child', *Human Rights Quarterly* 23, No. 2, 2001, pp. 308–326 and U. Kilkelly, *The Child and the European Convention on Human Rights* (Aldershot, Ashgate, 1999).

[66] Council of Europe, *Recommendation Rec(2005)5 of the Committee of Ministers to member states on the rights of children living in residential institutions*, adopted by the Committee of Ministers on 16 March 2005 at the 919th meeting of the Minister's Deputies.

the Parliamentary Assembly's Recommendation 1601(2003)[67] on improving the lot of abandoned children in institutions that are of relevance. Most importantly, the Council of Europe's Recommendation subsumes a whole range of different types of facilities under the term 'institution' and asserts that the best residential care setting is 'a small family-style living unit'.[68] It formulates certain 'principles and quality standards' that should be applied as widely as possible with regard to the placement of children in residential institutions.

41. The basic principles of the Council of Europe's Recommendation reaffirm that 'the family is the natural environment for the growth and well-being of the child' and state that 'preventive measures' should be taken to support children and families 'in accordance with their special needs'. It then formulates a set of principles that should apply to the placement of children, in particular the principle that placement in a residential institution should 'remain the exception' and that it should aim at the child's 'successful social integration or re-integration as soon as possible'. Furthermore, after-care support for a child leaving care should be guaranteed, the care setting should be regularly reviewed and, above all, the child's right to be heard in the review of the placement should be guaranteed (in accordance with the child's age and his or her degree of maturity). Of particular interest is the principle that 'all measures of control and discipline which may be used in residential institutions [. . .] should be based on public regulations and approved standards'. No such principle is explicitly formulated in the CRC, but it could clearly constitute one element for assessing the 'suitability' of a care setting.

42. The Council of Europe's Recommendation is of direct relevance to the issue of children deprived of their family environment inasmuch as it repeatedly stresses the importance of taking into account the child's views and 'wishes' and of giving the child possibilities to make him- or herself heard, both when decisions are taken as regards the child's placement in a residential institution *and* when reviewing the child's situation in this institution. Furthermore, it lists rights that have not been laid down in the CRC but seem to be of utmost relevance for the requirement to guarantee 'continuity in a child's upbringing' (Article 20(3) of the CRC) in case of deprivation of family environment. One such right, for example, is the 'right for

---

[67] Council of Europe, *Parliamentary Assembly Recommendation 1601 (2003)*, adopted by the Assembly on 2 April 2003 (13th Sitting).
[68] *Cf. supra* note 66.

siblings, whenever possible, to stay together or maintain regular contact'. This statement is of immediate relevance to the question of child-headed households, and recent reports on the situation of children without parental care have brought to light that, in many cases of separation of children from their families, public authorities did not ensure that siblings remain together, particularly when placed in institutional care. Similarly, children placed in foster care often cannot remain together with their siblings, unless the foster family agrees to care for more than one child.[69] Additionally, the Recommendation calls for 'an efficient system of monitoring and external control of residential institutions' and for 'relevant statistical data [. . .] and research for the purposes of efficient monitoring'. These efforts to adhere to standards and monitor children's situation in residential institutions should also, according to the Recommendation, apply to any non-governmental bodies that are involved with residential institutions.

3.3 Regional Case-Law: Decisions by the European Court of Human Rights

43. With regard to regional case-law, the European Court of Human Rights has produced a number of decisions that protect the interests of the child on the one hand and affirm the role of families in child care on the other (Article 8 of the European Convention on Human Rights and Fundamental Freedoms establishes the right of anyone 'to respect for his private and family life' – it is not a child-specific article). None of the articles of the European Convention on Human Rights contains specific provisions for children and minors, even though some articles – particularly Articles 3, 5 and 8 – might be applicable to the cases of intra-familial child abuse and, as such, form the basis for the removal of a child from his or her family environment.[70] It is particularly Article 8 that has engendered certain court cases of interest. The Court's decision in K.A. v. Finland (14 January 2003), for example, ruled that the Finnish authorities had violated Article 8 of the European Convention by failing to reunite children with their parents after they had been removed from their family environment on the allegation of sexual

---

[69] See for example I. Milligan, L. Hunter and A. Kendrick, *Current trends in the use of residential child care in Scotland* (Glasgow, Scottish Institute of Residential Child Care, 2006). Milligan *et al.* provide evidence that siblings are, in many cases, separated from each other, due to lack of facilities or incapacity of authorities.

[70] See particularly E. Dumitriu-Segnana, *Case Law of the European Court of Human Rights related to child rights, role of the families and alternative care* (paper presented at the International Conference on Child Rights, Bucharest, Romania, 2–3 February 2006).

abuse and placed in long-term public care. The Court was of the opinion that the children's removal had been lawful but that:

> '[t]he restricted contact between the biological parents and their children and the failure of the social welfare authorities to review that restriction genuinely and sufficiently frequently, far from facilitating a possible reunification, contributed to hindering it'.[71]

44. This judgement affirmed the right of the child to maintain regular contact with his or her natural family and the obligation of public authorities to spare no efforts to possibly reunite a child with his or her family after placement in a public care institution. Other cases before the European Court confirmed the Court's emphasis on the fact that for many children the removal from the family environment had been in the child's best interests but that all procedures that *followed* the removal had to take into account the rights of the child's biological parents to the maximum extent possible.[72] In these judgements the Court confirmed the positive obligation of States to reunite parents with their children and affirmed that removal from the family and placement in alternative care should always be considered as a temporary measure.[73] While these judgements basically referred to the rights of parents under Article 8, other judgements of the Court protected the right of the child to physical integrity. In *Scozzari and Giunta v. Italy* of 13 July 2000, the Court ruled that the temporary placement of children in residential care institutions whose heads had earlier been convicted of child abuse violated Article 8 of the European Convention on Human Rights.[74] It was the Court's opinion that public authorities had failed to assess carefully the suitability of the institutional care setting and, as such, had disregarded the best interests of the child.

45. Both the above-mentioned Recommendations of the Council of Europe and Parliamentary Assembly as well as the African Charter of the Rights of the Welfare of the Child are more explicit on certain aspects related to

---

[71] ECtHR, *K.A. v. Finland*, 14 January 2003.

[72] For example ECtHR, *B. v. United Kingdom*, 8 July 1987 and ECtHR, *K. and T. v. Finland*, 27 April 2000.

[73] E. Dumitriu-Segnana, *o.c.* (note 70), p. 4.

[74] For an account of recent developments in common law regarding the liability of public authorities for children abused in institutional care, see M. Hall, 'The Liability of Public Authorities for the Abuse of Children in Institutional Care: Common Law Developments in Canada and the United Kingdom', *International Journal of Law, Policy and the Family* 14, No. 3, 2000, pp. 281–301.

Article 20 of the CRC than the CRC itself. As such, these documents might help in defining the scope of Article 20. The African Charter puts a greater emphasis on those children deprived of their family environment by natural disaster or armed conflict: it includes an explicit reference to internally displaced children and stipulates that States Parties should take all necessary measures to reunite the child with his or her family. The Council of Europe Recommendation, for its part, provides a whole catalogue of requirements and standards that aim to a) safeguard the child's participation in any decisions regarding his or her placement in an institution as well as his or her situation *within* that institution, b) avoid the discrimination of the child in terms of life opportunities and c) ensure that placement in an institution should be a measure of last resort and, if applied, should not be longer than necessary.

4. *Monitoring Efforts and Reporting Guidelines*

46. Notwithstanding the scarcity of further international legislation against which Article 20 could be compared, the monitoring efforts and reporting guidelines issued by various treaty bodies point to the evidence that children who find themselves abandoned or deprived of their family environment are singled out as particularly vulnerable children. The recent UNHCR Guidelines on the Formal Determination of the Best Interests of the Child testify to an international consensus on the fact that 'higher procedural safeguards' are required for the determination of the best interests of children who find themselves living outside their family environment.[75] Thus, the various treaty bodies confirm that heightened attention should be paid to infringements of the rights of children deprived of a family environment, and that States Parties should introduce robust legislation on behalf of these children as well as give detailed information as to how the State is fulfilling its obligation to provide special assistance and protection to them.

47. While both Covenants, for example, merely underline that children in general are entitled to special care, protection and assistance, the reporting guidelines of both the CCPR and CESCR make it obvious that the situation of children deprived of their family environment is seen as particularly

---

[75] See UNHCR, *UNHCR Guidelines on the Formal Determination of the Best Interests of the Child* (Geneva, UNHCR, 2006), p. 9.

problematic and, thus, that implementation measures should also put emphasis on this group of children. In 1989, the Human Rights Committee issued a General Comment on Article 24 of the CCPR ('Rights of the Child') in which it explicitly calls upon States to give evidence of 'the special measures of protection adopted to protect children who are abandoned or deprived of their family environment in order to enable them to develop in conditions that most closely resemble those characterizing the family environment'.[76] In a similar vein, the (revised) reporting guidelines of the Committee on Economic, Social and Cultural Rights for Article 10 of the CESCR require States Parties to this treaty to indicate if, in their country, there are:

> '[. . .] any groups of children and young persons which do not enjoy the measures of protection and assistance at all or which do so to a significantly lesser degree than the majority. In particular, what is the respective situation of orphans, children without living biological parents, young girls, children who are abandoned or deprived of their family environment, as well as physically or mentally handicapped children?'[77]

48. To summarize: the discussion of existing human rights legislation potentially covering the situation of children without parental care as well as its comparison with Article 20 of the CRC demonstrate that both the value of the family as the most desirable environment for a child's upbringing as well as the fact that children living *outside* their family environment are particularly vulnerable, emerge as uncontested principles in international law. Yet, apart from the 1986 Declaration, international human rights legislation is incoherent with regard to how conflicts of interests between the child, his or her parents and the relevant State authorities are to be weighed and decided. Equally, in the CRC as elsewhere, there seems to be an apparent lack of specification as regards different forms of alternative care, mechanisms for monitoring and periodic review of alternative placements as well as procedures to safeguard the child's continuity in upbringing, minimal emotional disruption as well as non-discrimination in terms of life opportunities.

---

[76] Human Rights Committee, *o.c.* (note 41).

[77] CESCR Committee, *Revised general guidelines regarding the form and contents of reports to be submitted by states parties under articles 16 and 17 of the International Covenant on Economic, Social and Cultural Rights* (UN Doc. E/C.12/1991/1, 1991).

CHAPTER THREE

SCOPE OF ARTICLE 20

49. This chapter systematically examines the key concepts in the formulation of Article 20 in order to determine the situations it covers and the nature and extent of State obligations in their regard.

50. The first short section gives an overall insight into how the basic scope of Article 20 was determined, bringing together in one place the main features of the development of the text, various elements of which are discussed in more detail at appropriate points later in the chapter. In the second section, we examine in particular the interpretation and ramifications of terms used in order to define which children are to be the beneficiaries of the rights afforded. The third and final section looks at the substance of those rights and considerations for their implementation.

1. *Overview of the Drafting History*

51. Article VI of the initial Polish proposal submitted to the Commission on Human Rights in 1978 already targeted the specific situation and vulnerability of children living outside their family environment: 'Society and the public authorities shall have the duty to extend particular care to children without a family [. . .]'.[78] This principle was reiterated in Article 11 of the second Polish draft, which became the basic working document of the Informal Working Group for the Convention on the Rights of the Child. Interestingly, this article continued to be unofficially headed 'special protection measures for parentless children' until 1991, when it was reformulated by the CRC Committee as 'children deprived of a family environment'.[79] The change in wording to a less restrictive descriptor already indicates a significant shift in approach.

---

[78] First Polish Draft contained in ECOSOC, *1978 report of the Working Group to the Commission on Human Rights* (UN Doc. E/CN.4/1292, 1978).
[79] UNICEF, *o.c.* (note 2) (UN-SEC-HR/1996/SER.1/ARTICLE.20).

52. When the second Polish proposal was submitted to the Working Group in 1979, paragraph 2 of Article 11 defined the child covered by the article as 'a child deprived of his natural family environment'. Furthermore, the second Polish proposal emphasized the duty of States Parties to 'facilitate adoption and create favourable conditions for establishing foster families'. The proposals submitted thereafter, in the 1981 session of the Working Group, already expressed concern over this all-too-open call upon States Parties to provide for adoption possibilities. Australia stated that adoption should only be facilitated 'where appropriate', while Denmark went even further by stating that 'the child shall not, however, be adopted unless there has been a serious attempt to investigate and elucidate his status concerning parents, guardians, relatives and other biological and stable social relations'.

53. Until 1982, the proposals for Article 11 always addressed the child 'deprived of parental care'. This formulation was criticized at the 1982 session of the Working Group, when one speaker contended that it should be replaced by the term 'biological family'. However, this even more restrictive wording was immediately met by a counter-proposal that argued in favour of a broader formulation: 'natural family environment'. After some discussion and after India and the United States had introduced another compromise text, the formulation was changed to '*normal* family environment' [our emphasis]. Both the representatives of Brazil and the Byelorussian Soviet Socialist Republic suggested that the adjective 'normal' should be eliminated 'in order to avoid conceptual difficulties arising from the use of this term'.[80] When the representatives of France and the United States voiced their preference to speak of the child 'deprived of his family environment' rather than 'deprived of parental care', this terminology finally found its way into the draft CRC.

54. The emphasis on particular alternative solutions for children without parental care proved to be another contentious issue during the drafting of the CRC. While certain delegations' statements revealed that in their view the most desirable form of alternative care was 'permanent adoption of the child' (US delegation in 1982), others were more cautious with their support for adoption. It was also during the 1982 session of the Working Group that the delegation of India for the first time introduced a list of alternative care possibilities, '*inter alia,* foster placement, and placement in community and State child care institutions'.[81]

---

[80] *Ibid.*
[81] ECOSOC, *1982 report of the Working Group to the Commission on Human Rights*, (UN Doc. E/CN.4/1982/90/Add. 7, 1982), para. 51.

55. Following the introduction of a range of possible alternative care 'solutions', which was generally accepted by the other delegations, Australia finally proposed to insert the word 'suitable' before the words 'community or State child care institutions'.[82] This proposal was accepted without further discussion. It was not until the Second Reading that delegates suggested that a distinction be made between alternative *family-based* care, such as foster placements, and placement in institutions. A compromise text for Article 20, drafted by 12 delegations,[83] for the first time mentioned the tradition of '*kafala*' practised in many Islamic countries and, over and above that, inserted the term 'if necessary' preceding 'placement in suitable institutions'.[84] Thus, the compromise paragraph 20(3) introduced the subsidiarity of institutionalized alternative care. Thereafter, no delegation questioned the formulation 'if necessary', even though the ordering of potential alternative solutions was changed a few times.

56. In the end, it was the Venezuelan delegation that proposed an ordering of the alternative care-list that arranged the types of alternative care in a logical order that moved from the most temporary (foster placement) to the most permanent measure (adoption).[85] The qualifier 'if necessary' with regard to 'suitable institutions' was not included in the list. While the logic of ordering was generally accepted by the rest of the delegates, institutions were nevertheless singled out as a measure of last resort, so that the final wording of Article 20(3) read: 'Such care could include, *inter alia*, foster placement, *Kafala* of Islamic law, adoption, or if necessary placement in suitable institutions for the care of children'.

2. *Children Covered by Article 20*

2.1 *The Meaning of 'Family Environment'*

57. State obligations to provide special protection and assistance by ensuring alternative care under Article 20 come into play when a child is without his or her 'family environment'. Determining what constitutes this environment is therefore a key issue. What, for example, is the responsibility

---

[82] *Ibid.*, para. 55.

[83] Argentina, Australia, Brazil, China, France, Italy, the Netherlands, Pakistan, Sweden, the Union of Soviet Socialist Republics, the United Kingdom of Great Britain and Northern Ireland and Portugal.

[84] ECOSOC, *1989 report of the Working Group to the Commission on Human Rights*, (UN Doc. E/CN.4/1989/48, 1989), paras. 339–348.

[85] *Ibid.*, para. 347.

of the State to provide special protection and assistance to a child in informal kinship care, *i.e.* whose parent(s) have taken the initiative to place him or her within the extended family or who has spontaneously been taken in by relatives? Does a child-headed household of siblings qualify as a 'family environment' and could it therefore be argued that children in such a household might be excluded from receiving special protection and assistance? Questions such as these are not necessarily easy to resolve on the basis of the CRC itself.

58. It is first of all important to underline the fact that the reference in paragraph 1 of Article 20 is to 'his or her' family environment, and not to 'a' family environment. In this respect, it clearly tackles a different issue to that broached in the preamble where it is recognized that 'the child, for the full and harmonious development of his or her personality, should grow up in a family environment, in an atmosphere of happiness, love and understanding.' At the same time, of course, this preambular statement underlies both a potential justification for removing a child from parental care – where there is lack of 'happiness, love and understanding' – and the preference given to family-based alternative care solutions in paragraph 3 of Article 20, which is discussed below.

59. During the initial drafting phase (1980–1982) of Article 20, consideration was given to several proposals designed to clarify the scope of the provision, notably: deprived of 'parental care' (in the Polish revised draft), '[care of] parents or other members of [the] biological family', 'biological family', 'natural family environment', and 'normal family environment'. The final decision to accept the least prescriptive term 'his or her family environment' indicates both a wish to look further than simple parental care and the impossibility of trying to define more exactly the family.[86]

60. Not surprisingly, similar discussions took place in relation to the scope and terminology of several other provisions of the CRC where the role of parents or other caregivers vis-à-vis the child was to be determined. The fact that they resulted in a wide range of outcomes has clear repercussions for Article 20, both with regard to interpreting 'family environment' for the purpose of implementing this article, and to establishing the exact linkages among the various provisions. The spectrum of these references – ranging from the highly restrictive 'parents' alone to the broad inclusion of informal

---

[86] *Travaux Préparatoires* (UN Doc. E/1982/12/Add.1, C, pp. 56–59, 1982), reproduced in S. Detrick (ed.), *The United Nations Convention on the Rights of the Child. A Guide to the Travaux Préparatoires* (Dordrecht, Martinus Nijhoff, 1992), p. 298.

customary carers, according to the case – is illustrated by the following list of CRC provisions (our italics):

- a child has the right, as far as possible, to know and be cared for by his or her parents (Article 7) and not to be separated from them against their will, unless this is deemed to be in the child's best interests (Article 9);
- however, Article 18 ascribes the primary responsibility for the upbringing and development of the child to parents *or legal guardians*;
- while Article 3 adds a further element, obligating States to ensuring 'such protection and care as is necessary for [the child's] well-being, taking into account the rights and duties of his or her parents, *legal guardians, or other individuals legally responsible* for him or her';
- whereas under Article 27 parents *and others responsible for the child* – which would thus include, but not be limited to, those with fully-fledged legal responsibility – are to be assisted in securing the conditions of living necessary for the child's development;
- and Article 5 hints at what the general term 'others responsible' might denote, mentioning the 'responsibilities, rights and duties of parents or, where applicable, *the members of the extended family or community as provided for by local custom, legal guardians or other persons legally responsible for the child*'.

61. In the context of this Commentary, it is of special importance to look closely at the origin and significance of this last provision with its broad perspective on the family and others responsible for the child – the explicit reference therein to the 'extended family' is, moreover, unique in the CRC.

62. The proposal to formulate Article 5 in this way came at the Technical Review stage (1988) in a note from the Secretariat, which read:

> 'The draft Convention as a whole may not adequately recognize the role of the extended family and community when parental care is not available. Because cultures, traditions and customs in many countries and areas provide for such a role, the Working Group may wish to broaden Article [5] accordingly. Taking also into account the wording of Article [20], both paragraphs 1 and 2, which mention the "family environment" in a similar context, it would seem desirable to include in Article [5], as the relevant umbrella article, a reference to these circumstances. This might be accomplished by adding the words "the extended family or community as provided for by local custom" after the word "applicable".'[87]

---

[87] UN Secretariat, *Additional Comments and Clarifications* (UN Doc. E/CN.4/1989/WG.1/ CRP.1/Add.1, 1989), para. 13.

63. With the insertion of 'members of' before the words 'the extended family', this was the version adopted by the Working Group at Second Reading (1989).[88] It therefore took the scope of the article beyond persons with 'legal' responsibility, a stance reflected elsewhere in the CRC only in Article 27.

The Committee on the Rights of the Child has noted that:

> 'the Convention reflects different family structures arising from various cultural patterns and emerging familial relationships [and] refers to various forms of families, such as the extended family, and is applicable to a variety of families such as the nuclear family, re-constructed family, joint family, single-parent family, common-law family and adoptive family.'[89]

64. Referring to the tenor of the above-mentioned note from the Secretariat, some commentators have gone further, claiming that the concept in Article 5 indeed constitutes the baseline, or 'umbrella', for the Convention as a whole in this respect.[90] The validity of this standpoint, however, could be open to question on a number of counts including:

– there is no mention whatsoever in the *Travaux Préparatoires* of any discussion on the substantive or other merits of the reasoning contained in the note from the Secretariat and, in particular, of the possibility that Article 5 might be considered as an 'umbrella' article in this regard for the CRC as a whole, and no indication as to acceptance of this by the Working Group;
– the *Travaux Préparatoires* simply record that '[s]everal delegations voiced their support for the idea of giving recognition in the Convention to the notion of extended family or community responsibility for the child. While there was no *strong* opposition to [the proposed] *inclusion in Article [5]*, it was nevertheless argued that the introduction of this concept would change essentially the traditional triangular responsibility for the child.'[91] [our emphasis];
– despite the affirmation in the note from the Secretariat, there is no reason to suppose that the role of members of the extended family or community in a child's upbringing might in any way be restricted to

---

[88] *Travaux Préparatoires*, UN Doc. E/CN.4/1989/48, reproduced in S. Detrick (ed.), *o.c.* (note 86), p. 303.

[89] CRC Committee, *o.c.* (note 1), para. 6.

[90] See, for example Ph. Alston, 'The Best Interests Principle: Towards a Reconciliation of Culture and Human Rights', *International Journal of Law, Policy, and the Family* 8, No. 1, 1994, p. 11; G. Van Bueren, *The International Law on the Rights of the Child* (Dordrecht, Martinus Nijhoff, 1995), p. 71.

[91] S. Detrick (ed.), *o.c.* (note 86), p. 161.

situations where 'parental care is not available', in general or in terms of Article 5. In many cases, upbringing roles are shared by custom, within the wider family or beyond, and the direct link made between Articles 5 and 20 would therefore seem to have no clear – or at least exclusive – basis;

- the wide range of persons foreseen in Article 5 applies only to the very narrow and specific role of providing 'appropriate direction and guidance' for children in the exercise of their rights;
- Article 5 is not one of the four articles containing 'general principles', as defined by the CRC Committee, which are to underlie the CRC and its interpretation as a whole and in which the implementation of its various provisions is therefore to be grounded;[92]
- in contrast, Article 3 figures among those general principles and mentions, over and above parents, only 'legal guardians, or other individuals legally responsible' for the child. Since, in addition, it precedes Article 5 and deals far more explicitly and broadly with care issues, it might reasonably be considered to be more fundamental to the treaty;
- it is quite clear in the formulation of articles such as 3, 7, 9 and 18 that rights and duties are to be limited to, at the most, persons with legal responsibility for the child.

65. Nonetheless, it is reasonable to contend that the spirit in which Article 5 was phrased and adopted – one of cultural sensitivity and inclusiveness – should somehow find appropriate reflection in the interpretation of 'family' in Article 20. This corresponds, for example, to the approach taken by the Human Rights Committee in its General Comment No. 19 where it noted that:

'the concept of the family may differ in some respects from State to State, and even from region to region within a State, and that it is therefore not possible to give the concept a standard definition. [. . .] States parties should report on how the concept and scope of the family is construed or defined in their own society and legal system. Where diverse concepts of the family, 'nuclear' and 'extended', exist within a State, this should be indicated with an explanation of the degree of protection afforded to each. In view of the existence of various forms of family, such as unmarried couples and their children or single parents and their children, States parties should also indicate whether and to what extent such types of family and their members are recognized and protected by domestic law and practice.'[93]

---

[92] See CRC Committee, *Overview of the Reporting Procedure* (UN Doc. CRC/C/33, 1994); this document lists articles 2, 3, 6, and 12 as the 'guiding principles' of the CRC.

[93] Human Rights Committee, *o.c.* (note 42), para. 28.

66. In fact, it was in a slightly earlier General Comment by this same Committee on Article 24 of the CCPR that this issue was broached in a seemingly decisive manner, but in fact leaving some doubts for the interpretation of Article 20 of the CRC:

> 'it is primarily incumbent on the family, which is interpreted broadly to include all persons composing it in the society of the State party concerned, and particularly on the parents, to create conditions to promote the harmonious development of the child's personality and his enjoyment of the rights recognized in this Covenant. [. . .] [I]n cases where *the parents and the family* seriously fail in their duties, ill-treat or neglect the child, the State should intervene to restrict parental authority and *the child may be separated from his family* when circumstances so require.'[94] [our emphasis]

67. While accepting this approach in general terms, there still remains the problem of establishing the precise linkage between, in particular, removal from parental care foreseen under Article 9 and from the family environment under Article 20. The gap between the two is underlined by the absence of any reference in the CRC to the concept of 'kinship care'.

68. Whatever the country, most children without parental care are in reality looked after informally – and usually by members of the extended family, at the request of the parents or spontaneously.[95] Those providing informal kinship care of this kind in principle have no legal responsibility as such for the child. State obligations in regard to these care settings would certainly extend to protection of the child from all forms of abuse, neglect and exploitation 'while in the care of parent(s), legal guardians or any other person who has the care of the child' (Article 19(1) of the CRC), as well as to assist 'parents and others responsible for the child' in ensuring that the child has 'a standard of living adequate for the child's physical, mental, spiritual, moral and social development' (Article 27(1) of the CRC). Other guarantees applying to extra-familial placements – including their regulation by law and reviews of their necessity and appropriateness from all points of view (see below) – would not apply, however.

69. The no-man's-land between Articles 9 and 20 has furthermore been interpreted, more especially by default, as implying that in case the child is deprived of his/her parents or it is in his/her best interest to be removed

---

[94] Human Rights Committee, *o.c.* (note 41), para. 6.
[95] See for example G. Foster, 'The capacity of the extended family safety net for orphans in Africa', *Psychology, Health & Medicine* 5, No. 1, 2000, pp. 55–62.

from them, 'the State should first seek placement in the child's wider family, as defined in article 5, before looking for alternatives.'[96] This view is backed up by the text of the 1986 Declaration which specifies 'care by relatives of the child's parents' as being, implicitly, the first option to consider when 'care by the child's own parents is unavailable or inappropriate.'[97] In practice, formal placements by the child care authorities in many countries are indeed increasingly taking the form of 'kinship foster care'.[98] However, it should be recalled that, like any other form of alternative care, kinship care does not automatically constitute the most favourable option for every child and in every family situation – alongside the potential advantages, there are many risks and requirements that need to be fully evaluated on a case-by-case basis.[99] In other words, all obligations relating to alternative care in general must be respected where formal kinship care is envisaged or ordered, since the placement results from a decision by the State, either at its own initiative or in response to a proposal from the interested parties.

70. Bearing in mind all of the above considerations, we can conclude that the State has no obligation under Article 20 to ensure alternative care for a child who, for whatever reason, is not in the care of his or her parents but is being looked after by a member of the extended family, whether spontaneously or at the behest of the parents.

71. As far as Article 20 is concerned, there is no reason to suppose that the term 'his or her family environment' should automatically extend to non-relatives. Only if 'kinship care' is ordered or subsequently officialized by a competent authority does it qualify as a form of 'alternative care'. In that case, the State is then bound to apply all criteria and safeguards applicable to alternative care in general.

72. By implication, it is arguable that opportunities for kinship care should be given priority by the competent authorities when fulfilling their responsibilities to ensure alternative care. However, as noted above, State

---

[96] R. Hodgkin and P. Newell, o.c. (note 27), p. 259.

[97] Article 4 of the CRC.

[98] See, for example, regarding the USA: National Conference of State Legislatures, *State Child Welfare Legislation 2005*, Washington DC, July 2006; regarding Australia: Australian Institute of Family Studies, *Resource Sheet No. 8*, February 2005; regarding South Africa: South African Law Reform Commission, *Discussion Paper 103*, ch. 17, 2002; regarding New Zealand: Royal Australasian College of Physicians, *Health of children in "out-of-home" care*, Sydney, 2006.

[99] ISS/UNICEF, *Kinship care: an issue for international standards*, 2004, available at http://www.iss-ssi.org/Resource_Centre/Tronc_DI/documents/KinshipENG.pdf.

obligations then encompass all requirements related to decisions on appropriate alternative care.

73. Finally at this point, it should be emphasized that the State must be in a position to respond to its protective and supportive duties towards the child, in accordance with other provisions of the CRC, whether or not the child is in the care of his or her parents. A pre-requisite for this is that it be aware of the presence of the child in a care setting other than that of the parents. As a logical consequence, the State needs to encourage or require notification of kinship or other informal care arrangements made for a child not living with his or her parents.

2.2   Loss of, or Removal from, the Family Environment

74. Article 20 refers to the situation of any child who is either 'temporarily or permanently deprived of his or her family environment' or 'cannot be allowed to remain in that environment' in view of his or her best interests. This scope is considerably wider than the one reflected in the preamble to the 1986 Declaration, which mentions only 'children who are abandoned or become orphans owing to violence, internal disturbance, armed conflicts, natural disasters, economic crises or social problems'.[100]

75. In particular, coverage under Article 20 is extended to children who 'cannot be allowed to remain' with their family, notably those whose removal from parental care is envisaged under Article 9 – by decision of competent authorities and subject to judicial review. However, Article 9 concerns only those situations where the child's separation takes place against the will of the parents; there are also instances where the justification of a decision to remove a child is understood and accepted by the parents, and therefore in principle does not take place against their wishes. State obligations under Article 20 also extend to this group of children.

76. Although the term 'deprived of' might normally suggest a situation resulting from a deliberate act by a third party, it is clear from the context that the drafters intended it to cover not only removal or separation of a child from parental care, whether justified and lawful or not, but also any situation where a child is bereft of parental care, for whatever reason.

77. From a strictly grammatical standpoint, the phrase 'temporarily or permanently' in this provision applies only to the situation with which it is

---

[100] Preamble of the 1986 Declaration.

textually immediately linked, *i.e.* deprivation of family environment that is not the result of a decision by the competent authorities to remove the child from parental care. It does not appear to be the intention of the drafters, however, that the words 'cannot be allowed to remain' be interpreted only in a definitive sense. The subsequent mention of foster-care – a predominantly short- or medium-term measure – as one of the potential responses to, apparently, both kinds of situations (para. 3) is one indication that removal may also be seen as a temporary measure. Similarly, 'placement in suitable institutions' (para. 3) is equally applicable to both situations: being also subject to the 'periodic review' (Article 25) of its appropriateness and on-going necessity, it too is clearly to be envisaged as a potentially temporary care arrangement.

78. Consequently, and although there is no explicit indication here or elsewhere in the CRC itself that alternative care might be provided specifically for children removed temporarily from their family environment (and thus with a view to their eventual return to that environment), it is reasonable to suppose that this provision is applicable to all children not able or allowed to live in their family environment, for whatever length of time and for whatever reason. The reasons would include, but not be limited to:

- the death of the parents,
- relinquishment or abandonment by parents,
- parents being involuntarily untraceable,
- temporary or permanent incapacity of parents (imprisonment, illness, disability),
- voluntary placement by parents (for the child's medical or general care),
- the child's decision to leave or not return to the family home,
- the child's involuntarily internal displacement,
- arrival in a country as an unaccompanied minor seeking asylum or immigration, or as a victim of trafficking,
- an administrative or judicial decision to remove a child from parental care in his or her best interests (for protection and/or to ensure appropriate upbringing and care).

79. While non-exhaustive, this listing notably and very deliberately does not include children and young people who are deprived of their liberty or placed in a care setting as a result of a decision by a judicial or administrative authority consequent to their alleged or proven infringement of the law. There is certainly still some debate – not to say confusion – over the

extent to which juveniles in such situations might or should be covered by CRC provisions on alternative care. It is obviously true that their alleged or proven offence may lead to their being 'deprived of their family environment': responses to their situation often comprise support and protection measures, sometimes in a setting outside their family environment. However, the *Travaux Préparatoires* for Article 20 contain no mention whatsoever of discussion on such considerations, and responses to children in conflict with the law – and subject to placement orders as a result – are dealt with in detail elsewhere in the CRC and in other international instruments.[101] We willingly concede that some as yet unexplored overlap may exist in relation, particularly, with the mention of foster care and 'other alternatives to institutional care' in Article 40(4) of the CRC. Overall, however, we conclude that the drafters in no way had juveniles in conflict with the law in mind when formulating Article 20, and that State obligations in regard to their specific situation are, as therefore clearly intended, invariably to be dealt with on the basis and in the context of Articles 37 and 40 of the CRC.

80. A number of the situations in the listing in fact link directly to other more targeted provisions of the CRC that specify, to a greater or lesser extent, detailed obligations towards the children in question, such as for unaccompanied refugee children (Article 22); children with disabilities (Article 23); and child victims of trafficking (Articles 35 and 39). The relevant Commentaries should be consulted in these respects.

81. In contrast, several of the situations listed above concern 'recognized groups' of children whose particular needs are widely acknowledged and are frequently addressed in policy and programmes, but who are not explicitly mentioned in the CRC. These are, notably: children in child-headed households, homeless children (vagrant or 'street' children), children whose mother is in prison, internally displaced children and children outside their habitual country of residence.

82. For the first two of these groups, there are currently no other international instruments setting explicit standards or obligations, and it is therefore worthwhile looking more closely at how the obligations of Article 20 might apply in each case.

---

[101] Articles 37 and 40, especially 40(4) of the CRC. The other main instruments are the UN 'Beijing Rules' for the Administration of Juvenile Justice (*cf. supra* note 60) and the 'Havana Rules' for the Protection of Juveniles Deprived of their Liberty (*cf. supra* note 19).

2.2.1 Child-Headed Households

83. The phenomenon of children looking after one another following the loss of their parents – particularly in disaster and emergency situations – is not new. However, it had not been pinpointed for special attention at the time when the CRC was being drafted. Its incidence increased considerably during the Nineties, largely as a result of the ever-diminishing ability of the extended family and community to care for children orphaned by the HIV/AIDS pandemic, especially but not only in sub-Saharan Africa.[102]

84. While the State's overall CRC obligations clearly hold for children in such situations, the precise nature, extent and thrust of those obligations under Article 20 have yet to be clarified. There are two main issues that need to be resolved in order for such clarification to take place.

85. First is the definition of the term 'child-headed households' itself. In recent years, the widely-accepted view that these households are formed of sibling groups, headed by the oldest child, has been contested as being too narrow to reflect reality. It is argued that, although this is the prevalent form, there are other significant manifestations of situations where a child takes responsibility for others, such as cousins or even unrelated children from the wider community. It is also pointed out that children may have *de facto* responsibility for day-to-day decision-making in a household when parents are incapacitated, and therefore be its effective 'head'. In addition, even the concept of 'household' itself, in such circumstances, may require further examination: rather than involving a shared dwelling or 'roof', in the opinion of some commentators it might be defined better as, for example, a group of persons 'who eat from the same pot'.[103]

86. Second, there is debate as to whether child-headed households should be considered first and foremost as a type of 'family', and therefore approached from a family-preservation perspective, or primarily as a form of alternative care that enables family and other ties to be maintained. So far, it is in South Africa that this issue has been the most extensively reviewed, in the context of a legislative reform process. The outcome to date, while not entirely clear-cut, tends towards the second of these options: legally

---

[102] UNAIDS, UNICEF and USAID, *Children on the Brink* (New York, UNICEF, 2004).

[103] For discussion on definitions, see for example: M. MacLellan, 'Child Headed Households: Dilemmas of Definition and Livelihood Rights' (paper presented at the 4th World Congress on Family Law and Children's Rights, Cape Town, South Africa, March 2005) and S. Rosa, *Counting on Children. Realising the right to social assistance for child-headed households in South Africa* (Cape Town, University of Cape Town, 2004).

recognizing child-headed households as a care setting for children without parental care, which is to be supported and protected by an officially designated 'mentor'.[104]

87. The CRC Committee has not addressed these questions directly. However, noting that '[s]pecial attention must be given to children orphaned by AIDS and to children from affected families, including child-headed households',[105] it states:

> 'Orphans are best protected and cared for when efforts are made to enable siblings to remain together, and in the care of relatives or family members. [. . .] Assistance must be provided so that, to the maximum extent possible, children can remain within existing family structures. This option may not be available due to the impact HIV/AIDS has on the extended family. In that case, States parties should provide, as far as possible, for family-type alternative care (*e.g.* foster care). States parties are encouraged to provide support, financial and otherwise, when necessary, to child-headed households. . .'[106]

88. Implicitly, this approach seems to set child-headed households apart from 'alternative care' as such. However, the relationship to obligations under Article 20 remains unclear. On the one hand, the sibling group might be considered to constitute a 'family environment' within which it is deemed in the children's best interests that they stay, and this would in principle preclude consideration under Article 20. On the other hand, the 'special attention' and 'support' to be afforded to such households, together with the eventuality of envisaging 'family-type alternative care' for their members, correspond to the terms of this Article.

89. Overall, then, it seems that the basis on which rights may be claimed by those living in child-headed households has yet to be clearly determined. For the moment, these households remain somewhat in a no-man's-land as far as Article 20 at least is concerned.

2.2.2   Homeless Children (Vagrant or 'Street' Children)

90. As is the case for child-headed households, while State obligations under the CRC towards children living on the street – some in situations that might in fact be considered as constituting a child-headed household – are no less

---

[104] South African Law Commission, 'Review of the Child Care Act', Discussion Paper 103, 13 February 2002.

[105] CRC Committee, *General Comment No. 3, HIV/AIDS and the right of the child* (UN Doc. CRC/GC/2003/3, 2003), para. 31.

[106] *Ibid.*, para. 34.

than for any other child, the desired response to their situation is unclear both from the treaty itself and because of lack of guidance in other international legal texts.

91. Indeed, just two years after the CRC's entry into force, the United Nations General Assembly seems to have identified this inadequacy, taking the unusual step of expressing its particular concern on this point. While recognizing that 'strict compliance with the provisions of the Convention on the Rights of the Child constitutes a significant step towards solving the problems of street children', the General Assembly specifically invited 'the Committee on the Rights of the Child to consider the possibility of a general comment on street children'.[107] The Committee not having reacted positively to this suggestion to date, this issue – especially as it relates to the interpretation of obligations under Article 20 – ostensibly remains as unclear in 2006 as it was deemed to be in 1992.

92. Furthermore, strictly from the point of view of 'alternative care' as envisaged in Article 20, there are indications – in part by default – that this is not considered to be of special relevance to children living on the street. When formulating concluding observations regarding the situation of 'street children' in given countries, the CRC Committee has in recent times variously urged that attention be given, *inter alia*, to 'shelter', 'housing', 'accommodation', access to basic services and protection, and support for family reunification. While such references can be said to correspond to the duty of the State to provide 'special protection and assistance' under the terms of Article 20, no explicit or specific proposals are made as to consideration of concrete alternative care measures envisaged in this Article.[108]

93. Consequently, there would seem to be no clear basis at present for interpreting the overall pertinence of 'alternative care' under Article 20 for children living in the street.

94. For the three remaining groups of children mentioned above, in contrast, some guidance does exist in the CRC itself and in other instruments. These are analyzed for each group, below.

---

[107] UN General Assembly, *Resolution on the Plight of Street Children*, G.A. res. 47/126, 47 U.N. GAOR Supp. (No. 49)(U.N. Doc. A/47/49, 1992), para. 200.
[108] See, for example, CRC Committee, *Concluding Observations: Benin* (UN Doc. CRC/C/BEN/CO/2, 2006), para. 74; *Ethiopia* (UN Doc. CRC/C/ETH/CO/3, 2006), para. 70; *Jordan* (UN Doc. CRC/C/JOR/CO/3, 2006), para. 91; *Senegal* (UN Doc. CRC/C/SEN/CO/2, 2006), para. 59.

2.2.3   *Children Whose Mothers are in Prison*[109]

95. Refusal to allow a child to remain with his or her mother subject to a custodial measure falls under the general scope of Article 9 of the CRC, thus relying on the determination of the best interests of the child concerned and requiring that he or she be able to 'maintain personal relations and direct contact with both parents on a regular basis'. At present, practice in this regard – and therefore interpretation of the best interests of the child – varies widely throughout the world, ranging from total prohibition of children remaining with their mothers to formal or informal arrangements whereby children may remain up to age six or even older.[110]

96. If separation is decided, clearly the State must then assume all obligations set out in Article 20. If, on the contrary, the child is permitted to remain with the mother, a relevant provision is found in the 1955 UN Standard Minimum Rules for the Treatment of Prisoners which stipulates – in Rule 23 (2) – that '[w]here nursing infants are allowed to remain in the institution with their mothers, provision shall be made for a nursery staffed by qualified persons, where the infants shall be placed when they are not in the care of their mothers'.[111]

97. For its part, the African Charter contains a separate article on 'children of imprisoned mothers' which provides for 'special treatment to expectant mothers and to mothers of infants and young children who have been accused or found guilty of infringing the penal law'.[112] In addition to specifying that non-custodial measures should be preferred for such mothers, it obligates States Parties to 'establish special alternative institutions for holding such mothers' and to 'ensure that a mother shall not be imprisoned with her child'. The Charter therefore implicitly differentiates between a mother's deprivation of liberty (in a special institution) and her imprisonment, but does not indicate the features of a 'special alternative institution' that would render it appropriate for child care.

---

[109] For a discussion of the emotional consequences of child separation because of imprisonment of a parent, particularly his or her mother, see for example G. Doherty, *The Long-Term Effects of Non-Parental Child Care* (Toronto, University of Toronto, 1996), Chapter II on 'Non-parental child care before age one'.

[110] UNICEF ICDC, *Innocenti Digest No. 3: Juvenile Justice* (Florence, UNICEF ICDC, 1998); see also R. Taylor, *Women in Prison and Children of Imprisoned Mothers* (Geneva, Quaker United Nations Office, 2004).

[111] United Nations Standard Minimum Rules for the Treatment of Prisoners, adopted 30 August 1955 (UN Doc. A/CONF/611, annex I, E.S.C. res. 663C, 24 U.N. ESCOR Supp. (No. 1) at 11, UN Doc. E/3048 (1957)).

[112] Article 30 of the African Charter on the Rights and Welfare of the Child.

98. In a similar vein, the Parliamentary Assembly of the Council of Europe (PACE) has noted both that '[e]xperts agree that early maternal separation causes long-term difficulties' and that 'the development of young babies is retarded by restricted access to varied stimuli in closed prisons'.[113] Council of Europe Member States are therefore invited first of all 'to recognize that custody for pregnant women and mothers of young children should only ever be used as a last resort', but also 'to develop small scale secure and semi-secure units with social services support for the small number of mothers who do require such custody, where children can be cared for in a child-friendly environment'.

99. The diversity of national policies and practice demonstrates a lack of consensus not only in regard to the age until which young children should without question remain in their mother's care, but also regarding minimum conditions under which it can be deemed appropriate that children so remain and the degree to which efforts should be made to avoid custodial sentences for such mothers. As far as implementation of Article 20 itself is concerned, however, it could be said that these questions have only indirect impact, in that its obligations apply only to a child who, justifiably or not, is removed from his or her detained mother's care and for whom informal care arrangements have not been made within his or her family.

2.2.4 *Internally Displaced Children*
100. In essence, internally displaced persons (IDPs) are to enjoy 'the same rights and freedoms under international and domestic law as do other persons in their country',[114] and the CRC as such would therefore normally suffice in relation to internally displaced children. The drafters of the African Charter deemed it wise, however, to recognize explicitly that internally displaced children have the same rights, *mutatis mutandis*, as refugee children, one of which being that:

> 'Where no parents, legal guardians or close relatives can be found, the child shall be accorded the same protection as any other child permanently or temporarily deprived of his family environment for any reason.'[115]

---

[113] Council of Europe, Parliamentary Assembly, *Mothers and Babies in Prison*, Recommendation 1469(2000), adopted on 30 June 2000.

[114] UN Office of the Coordination of Humanitarian Affairs, *Guiding Principles on Internal Displacement* (contained in annex to UN Doc. E/CN.4/1998/53/Add.2,11 Feb 1998) (OCHA Guiding Internal Displacement Principles).

[115] Article XXIII(4) of the African Charter on the Rights and Welfare of the Child.

101. Because of the specific problems IDPs may encounter, moreover, it has been found necessary to develop Guiding Principles on Internal Displacement (GPID).[116] This text contains references to the special situation of children, their care and their links with their families. Thus, GPID Principle 4.2 stipulates that '[c]ertain internally displaced persons, such as children, especially unaccompanied minors, [. . .] shall be entitled to protection and assistance required by their condition and to treatment which takes into account their special needs.' This principle echoes the 'special protection and assistance' provision in Article 20.

102. The GPID go on to specify that '[t]he authorities undertaking such displacement shall ensure, to the greatest practicable extent, that [. . .] members of the same family are not separated'[117] and that '[f]amilies which are separated by displacement should be reunited as quickly as possible.'[118] In addition, '[m]embers of internally displaced families whose personal liberty has been restricted by internment or confinement in camps shall have the right to remain together.'[119]

103. It follows that Article 20 will come into play for internally displaced children if they have become separated from family members and until they are reunited with them.

2.2.5 *Children Outside Their Country of Residence*
104. Since the CRC is applicable to every child under a State's jurisdiction, obligations under Article 20 apply to children present but not habitually resident in that State who are without parental care, regardless of why the child is there and of his or her legal status. Such children may include refugees, asylum seekers, migrants and victims of trafficking, as well as those who are 'hosted' abroad under respite care and holiday schemes or during specialized medical treatment.

105. Notwithstanding its Article 22 (covering children who are seeking refugee status or who are considered refugees) and the general obligation under Article 39 regarding the recovery and social reintegration of child victims of neglect, exploitation or abuse, the CRC does not broach in any detail the issue of alternative care for these children.

---

[116] UNHCR Guiding Principles on Internal Displacement of 11 February 1998 (UN Doc. E/CN.4/1998/53/Add. 2, 1998).
[117] OCHA Guiding Internal Displacement Principle 7(2).
[118] OCHA Guiding Internal Displacement Principle 17(3).
[119] OCHA Guiding Internal Displacement Principle 17(4).

106. Interpreting obligations in their respect has been significantly helped by the adoption and entry into force of the 1996 Hague Convention on Protection of Children[120] which sets out the framework and criteria for determining the responsibilities – and limits on action – of States Parties towards children who are outside their country of habitual residence. It has important ramifications for protective responses in almost all cases of children's cross-border movement. Among the spheres to which it explicitly applies in such cases are:

- 'the designation and functions of any person or body having charge of the child's person or property, representing or assisting the child' (Article 3(d))
- 'the placement of a child in a foster family or in institutional care, or the provision of care by *kafala* or an analogous institution' (Article 3(e))
- 'the supervision by a public authority of the care of a child by any person having charge of the child' (Article 3(f)).[121]

107. Its provisions, building on those of the CRC, constitute a guide, framework and benchmark for international cooperation in this field:

'The 1996 Convention has uniform rules determining which country's authorities are competent to take the necessary measures of protection [of children at risk in cross-frontier situations]. These rules, which avoid the possibility of conflicting decisions, give the primary responsibility to the authorities of the country where the child has his or her habitual residence, but also allow any country where the child is present to take necessary emergency or provisional measures of protection. [. . .] The cooperation procedures within the Convention can be helpful in the increasing number of circumstances in which minors cross borders and find themselves in vulnerable situations in which they may be subject to exploitation and other risks. [. . .] The Convention provides for cooperation between States in relation to the growing number of cases in which children are being placed in alternative care across frontiers, for example under fostering or other long-term arrangements falling short of adoption.'[122]

108. Thus, notably as concerns questions dealt with under Article 20 of the CRC, the 1996 Convention stipulates that:

---

[120] Hague Conference on Private International Law, *Convention on Jurisdiction, Applicable Law, Recognition, Enforcement and Cooperation in Respect of Parental Responsibility and Measures for Protection of Children*, concluded 19 October 1996.

[121] However, this treaty does not cover, *inter alia*, the establishment or contesting of a parent-child relationship (Article 4(a)) or decisions on adoption, measures preparatory to adoption, or the annulment or revocation of adoption (Article 4(b)).

[122] W. Duncan, 'The Hague Convention of 19 October 1996 on Jurisdiction, Applicable Law, Recognition, Enforcement and Co-operation in Respect of Parental Responsibility and Measures for the Protection of Children,' *The Judges' Newsletter*, Vol. 6, Hague Conference on Private International Law, Autumn 2003, pp. 68–72.

'In all cases of urgency, the authorities of any Contracting State in whose territory the child [...] is present have jurisdiction to take any necessary measures of protection.'

'The measures taken under the preceding paragraph with regard to a child habitually resident in a Contracting State shall lapse as soon as the authorities which have jurisdiction [...] have taken the measures required by the situation.'[123]

In addition:

'If an authority having jurisdiction [...] contemplates the placement of the child in a foster family or institutional care, or the provision of care by *kafala* or an analogous institution, and if such placement or such provision of care is to take place in another Contracting State, it shall first consult with the Central Authority or other competent authority of the latter State. To that effect it shall transmit a report on the child together with the reasons for the proposed placement or provision of care.

The decision on the placement or provision of care may be made in the requesting State only if the Central Authority or other competent authority of the requested State has consented to the placement or provision of care, taking into account the child's best interests.'[124]

109. In sum, the terms of the 1996 Hague Convention on Protection of Children give a clear indication of the conditions under which provision of alternative care is to be ensured by any given State if the child concerned is, for whatever reason, elsewhere than in his or her country of habitual residence.

2.3   Best Interests of the Child

110. Article 20 is one of several in the context of which the general principle contained in Article 3 – that 'the best interests of the child shall be a primary consideration' in all actions concerning children – is explicitly repeated.[125] However, in this case, the repetition is not designed to emphasize the special importance of its application with regard to the issue under discussion, but to establish a clear link with the removal of the child from parental care, necessitated by his or her best interests, as foreseen and specified under Article 9.

---

[123] Article 11.

[124] Article 33.

[125] In this regard the UNHCR has also developed Guidelines on the 'Formal Determination of the Best Interests of the Child', in which it is stated that 'higher procedural safeguards' for the determination of the child's best interests are necessary for children growing up outside their family environment. See UNHCR, *o.c.* (note 75).

111. It is interesting that no special mention of 'best interests' was made (or even proposed, for that matter) in relation to decision-making regarding alternative care options. This seems all the more significant in that the preamble of the 1986 Declaration stipulates that 'in all foster placement and adoption procedures the best interests of the child should be the paramount consideration.' The same formulation – 'the paramount consideration' – is used again in Article 5 of the 1986 Declaration which, moreover, since it covers 'all matters relating to the placement of a child outside the care of the child's own parents', has a potentially wider application than to foster care and adoption alone. Of note too, is the fact that, unusually, this provision in the 1986 Declaration indicates specific elements on the basis of which the child's best interests might be determined: 'particularly his or her need for affection and right to security and continuing care'.

112. Given that the term 'the paramount' clearly constitutes a far higher standard than 'a primary' as contained in the general principle of Article 3 of the CRC, it might have logically been reproduced in Article 20 in relation to decisions on foster care and, by extension, on other forms of alternative care that could not be covered within the limited focus of the 1986 Declaration. The failure to do so is all the more striking in that the paramount nature of the best interests of the child is indeed recognized, in line with the 1986 Declaration, as far as adoption is concerned (Article 21).

113. Decision-making under Article 20 regarding the choice of initial alternative care setting and, bearing in mind Article 25, pursuant to review of its appropriateness and necessity, is therefore subject to the obligation of giving primary consideration to the child's best interests. However, since the essential validity of the non-binding principles contained in the 1986 Declaration is in no way diminished by the obligations set out in the CRC, the exhortation (as opposed to a requirement) to give paramountcy to these interests, in relation at least to foster care, remains intact.

3. Ensuring and Deciding among Care Options

3.1 Entitlement to 'Special Protection and Assistance Provided by the State'

114. The term 'special protection and assistance' is frequently used in both human rights and humanitarian law to describe the necessary response to the temporary or permanent needs of given groups that are particularly vulnerable because of their situation (*e.g.* refugee) or status (*e.g.* child) or both (*e.g.* child refugee). In the context of Article 20, it implies targeted

measures of protection and assistance over and above those required for children in general, and adapted to the specific situation of those without parental care, in order to compensate for their special vulnerability and thereby to enable their overall rights to be fulfilled.

115. The obligation to 'provide' is among the most constraining requirements made of a State in international law.[126] In the context of Article 20, it indicates the State's direct, active and absolute responsibility to furnish special protection and assistance to the child, as opposed to 'ensuring', or satisfying itself, that the necessary action is being taken. This would normally imply that the State must in all cases be the direct service provider,[127] but at the very least it would mean that the State is responsible for determining, making available and overseeing the effective use of all necessary resources for guaranteeing that the required services are provided in the event that it delegates any task involved to a non-State agency.

3.2 'In Accordance with Their National Laws'

116. Reference to domestic law is well-established in international human rights treaties inasmuch as States both retain all power to legislate in ways that do not reduce the rights they contain and need to take legislative measures (*cf.* Article 4 of the CRC) to ensure that those same rights are promoted and protected nationally. Indeed, sixteen other articles in the CRC make reference in one way or another to domestic law provisions.[128]

117. Mention of national laws in the context of Article 20 would seem to be motivated by three particular considerations. First, the 1986 Declaration stipulates that '[f]oster placement of children should be regulated by law' (Article 10), and by implication this would apply to all forms of extra-familial alternative care including those not covered by that Declaration. Second, it suggests the obligation to legislate on alternative care provision by both

---

[126] See, for example, CESCR Committee, *General Comment No. 12 on the right to adequate food*: 'The right to adequate food, *like any other human right*, imposes three types or levels of obligations on States Parties: the obligations to respect, to protect and to fulfil. In turn, the obligation to fulfil incorporates both an obligation to facilitate *and an obligation to provide.*' [our emphasis] (UN Doc E/CN.4/Sub.2/1999/12, 1992), para. 15.

[127] See, for example, U. Kracht, 'A human rights-based approach to food and nutrition development – Reflections from the ACC/Sub-Committee on Nutrition', presentation at workshop during 17th International Congress on Nutrition, Vienna, August 2001, cited in World Food Summit – 5 years later, 10–13 June 2002, FAO, at http://www.fao.org/worldfoodsummit/ sideevents/papers/y6667e.htm

[128] Articles 1, 7, 8, 9, 10, 12, 13, 14, 15, 16, 21, 22, 26, 37, 40 and 41 of the CRC.

public and private entities or persons. Third, it provides each State the necessary leeway to institute and recognize different forms of care and not to allow or recognize others. The obvious example in this instance relates to *kafala* and adoption (see below).

3.3 'Ensure Alternative Care'

118. The State's obligation to ensure alternative care does not imply that the care itself must be provided by a public structure, facility or employee, but this phrasing requires that the State take active steps to satisfy itself that each child requiring alternative care receives it. It is therefore permissible for care-giving to be delegated to a non-State entity, whether or not for-profit. However, in that case, the State must make certain that such care is then effectively provided and that, in all cases, it meets the standards laid down for the public and private sectors alike.[129]

3.4 'Such Care Could Include, Inter Alia'

119. The drafters took great pains to ensure that the forms of alternative care cited in Article 20 are not seen as an exclusive listing: the use of the term 'could include', which alone already clearly indicates both the optional nature and non-exclusivity of those care forms specified, is unambiguously bolstered by the mention of '*inter alia*' immediately afterwards.

120. Interestingly, the equivalent French rendition is considerably less conclusive in this respect, saying simply that 'Such substitute care may notably take the form of...' [our translation], and thus tending rather to emphasize the importance of the types of care cited than the idea that they constitute a list of examples among many.

121. Nonetheless, it seems evident that the intention was very much to leave open the kinds of alternative care provision that might be envisaged.

3.5 'Foster Placement, Kafala of Islamic Law, Adoption'

122. This evidence is borne out, *inter alia*, by the fact that the family-based options cited in Article 20 constitute only a sample of the known possibilities available, and seemingly deliberately so. Thus, for example, the drafters did not consider it necessary to mention explicitly the Iraqi *el dham* system,

---

[129] Article 3(3) of the CRC.

even though it was specified during the debates that this was not the same as either foster placement or *kafala*.[130] The latter was nonetheless incorporated in *extremis* – at the second reading stage in 1989 – having been recognized in the preamble of the 1986 Declaration of Principles as the principal counterpart to adoption, which Islamic law does not recognize. In this way, the Convention's acknowledgement of, and applicability to, diverse legal and cultural realities was demonstrated.

123. The inclusion of adoption itself in this listing deserves comment. From many standpoints, adoption could in fact be considered more as a potential outcome to be sought for a child in alternative care than a form of such care *per se*. It would therefore be more on a par with reintegration into the parental home than with foster care in that, once adopted, a child once again has parental care. This distinction is reinforced by the fact that alternative care placements with, for example, foster families, and in institutions, are to be subject to periodic review (Article 25), whereas adoption clearly is not.

124. Neither adoption nor foster care figured in the original Polish proposal, but were introduced side-by-side in its revised text (1980), according to which States would have had to 'undertake measures so as to facilitate adoption of children and create favourable conditions for establishing foster families.'[131] Not only was this connection never subsequently questioned during the drafting, but also the promulgation of the 1986 Declaration ostensibly reinforced the linkage by dealing exclusively with 'foster placement and adoption'. Article 11 of this Declaration, however, both indicates the nature of the relationship between the two practices and, particularly significantly, actually underlines the parity between adoption and family reintegration: '*Foster family care, though temporary in nature,* may continue, if necessary, until adulthood but *should not preclude either prior return to the child's own parents or adoption.*' [our emphasis] The fact that the specificities of adoption are dealt with separately and in detail in Article 21 of the CRC only serves to comfort further the position that adoption does not have its proper place in the CRC simply as one of a number of alternative care options as set out in Article 20.

---

[130] *Travaux Préparatoires*, UN Doc. E/CN.4/1989/48, para. 341, quoted in S. Detrick (ed.), *o.c.* (note 86), p. 303.

[131] *Travaux Préparatoires*, Basic working text as adopted by the 1980 Working Group (UN Doc. E/CN.4/1349, 1980), reproduced in S. Detrick, *o.c.* (note 86), p. 297.

125. As noted elsewhere in this Commentary,[132] while the circumstances in which the obligation to provide alternative care are broadly covered by the CRC, the latter does not give any specific guidance regarding the basis on which a given care option is to be decided – except, under Article 21, as concerns adoption – or any indication of the desirable aims of an alternative care placement. Had it done so, adoption might have been ascribed in a clearer manner the role that it is called upon to play: providing a stable, permanent and family-based solution as an appropriate outcome for some children who are in alternative care.

3.6 'Or if Necessary Placement in Suitable Institutions for the Care of Children'

126. However wise the approach of non-exclusivity in the listing of care options, it leaves unanswered the question of what the word 'institutions' was intended to cover. On the one hand, 'institutions' is the only non-family-based form of care that is mentioned, but already in the Eighties the term had the sole connotation in many quarters of undesirably large and impersonal establishments. On the other hand, no mention is made of any of the numerous intermediate care options, lying between 'institutions' of that kind and family-based settings, that were operational and/or being developed at that time, in the form of small residential units such as, for example, family-type homes or group homes. The question posed, then, is the extent to which 'institutions' was intended as a virtual synonym of 'residential care' or as a more restrictive concept.

127. The likely answer lies not in the *Travaux Préparatoires* but implicitly in the fact that the word 'suitable' was inserted to qualify 'institution': if the latter is suitable, then by definition the scope of the term cannot be restricted to those that are generally considered not to be. Indeed, the French version of Article 20 avoids the word '*institution*', using the possibly more neutral term '*établissements*' ('establishments' or 'facilities') instead.

128. This wider view is, moreover, clearly the one espoused by the recent Recommendation to Member States on Children's Rights in Residential Institutions, adopted by the Committee of Ministers of the Council of Europe.[133] Despite 'institutions' in its title, its own second guideline in fact specifies that placement should be in 'a small family-style living unit', a kind of facility

---

[132] See particularly Chapter III, Section 2.
[133] *Cf. supra* note 66.

that, in the minds of most, would not readily be associated with an institutional setting as such, but which could be eminently 'suitable'.

129. The position of 'institutions' as the last example of alternative care options, as well as being the only one qualified by the term 'if necessary', would seem to reflect a deliberate desire on the part of the drafters to relegate institutional placements to the status of 'last resort'. This view is corroborated by examination of the drafting history.

130. The original Polish proposal contained no examples of what the provision of 'particular care to children without a family' might entail. The corresponding part of the text of the revised proposal was similarly silent on what could constitute an 'appropriate educational environment [for] a child who is deprived of his natural family environment'.[134] While the next draft paragraph mentioned, as noted above, measures 'to facilitate adoption of children and create favourable conditions for establishing foster families', this was subsequently dropped.

131. But of special significance is the fact that, up to that moment, the specific question of residential care in general, or institutions in particular, had not been raised at all in the basic texts or during the debate. In fact, it was a compromise proposal by India and the US (1982) that first mentioned 'institutions' and, in so doing, provided the first working basis for what would become the finally approved text, proposing 'alternative family care which would include, *inter alia*, foster placement, and placement in community and State child care institutions.'[135]

132. Ensuing debate (1982) resulted in this final phrase being modified to read '*or* placement in *suitable* institutions for the care of children' [our emphasis], as well as 'could' being substituted for 'would'. This was the formulation maintained in the text subsequently adopted at the first reading (1987), and the Technical Review made no comment on this issue.

133. It was thus only at the moment of the second reading (1989) that, among other proposals, the insertion of the words 'if necessary' before 'placement in suitable institutions' (as well as the reference to *kafala*) was suggested, clearly inspired by the 1986 Declaration of Principles, which

---

[134] *Travaux Préparatoires* (UN Doc. E/CN.4/1349); reproduced in S. Detrick (ed.), *o.c.* (note 86), p. 297.

[135] *Travaux Préparatoires* (UN Doc. E/1982/12/Add. 1, C, 1982), para. 54; reproduced in S. Detrick (ed.), *o.c.* (note 86), p. 299.

contains the same qualifying term before 'by an appropriate institution'. It met with no opposition.

134. There was also discussion regarding the order in which the care options should be mentioned, and it is very illustrative of the prevailing tendency. In this context, and at a very late stage, Venezuela proposed the following: 'daily care, foster placement in its various forms, suitable institutions for the care of children, *kafala* and adoption'. This was aimed at reflecting 'the logical order of measures to be taken for the different degrees of family deprivation: starting with measures for children temporarily deprived of their family and ending with *kafala* and adoption, for children permanently and lawfully deprived of their family environment',[136] and significantly omitted the term 'if necessary'. This proposed re-ordering, however, elicited no reaction, indicating the drafters' active wish to maintain 'institutions' in an unequivocally marginal position. As a result, and in a similar vein, the general guidelines for periodic reports drawn up by the CRC Committee request indications of how States ensure that placements 'in suitable institutions will only be used if really necessary.'

135. Unfortunately, this view militates against the idea of establishing a range of care options, all of whose 'suitability' and 'necessity' are to be determined more particularly with reference to their ability to respond effectively and appropriately to the specific circumstances, needs and wishes of an individual child at a given time in his or her life, rather than on the basis of a pre-determined hierarchy of an ascribed intrinsic fitness to do so. When seeking to determine the best alternative care option, few would deny that opportunities within the extended family or in other family-based settings should be considered first. But, in doing so, there is a fundamental and vital difference between examining the options on a scale that runs from best to worst, and that of evaluating them in terms of how each might correspond to the child's needs at the time. It is widely recognized that, because of their experiences or particular characteristics, 'some children will always need institutional care'.[137] In this respect, it is worth noting that Article 21 uses the term 'suitable care', without making any distinction among the possible settings involved, when defining in-country care solutions

---

[136] *Travaux Préparatoires* (UN Doc. E/CN.4/1989/48); reproduced in S. Detrick (ed.), *o.c.* (note 86), p. 304.

[137] Parliamentary Assembly of the Council of Europe, *The rights of children in institutions: follow-up to Recommendation 1601 (2003) of the Parliamentary Assembly*, Recommendation 1698 (2005).

that preclude the need for recourse to intercountry adoption. In other words, for example, foster care too has to be assessed as to its suitability and necessity: serial breakdowns in foster placements are but one indication that it is not suitable for some children.[138] Thus, if an institution can be deemed 'suitable', and the child's placement there 'necessary', there may be grounds for questioning why that solution would automatically be relegated to 'last resort' status.

136. In sum, the term 'if necessary' is in practice invariably interpreted and justified more from the standpoint of the system ('nothing else is available') than from the standpoint of the child ('at this moment, this will best meet the child's needs'). As a result, 'if necessary' is seen to qualify an intrinsically undesirable care option to be used only for want of better. This surely does not constitute a constructive way of approaching potential alternative care solutions for any child. In contrast, the undoubtedly positive ramification of this wording is that it provides a stimulus and justification for de-institutionalization efforts. The concluding observations of the CRC Committee illustrate the systematic manner in which it seizes on this in order to urge States Parties to work towards that end.

3.6.1 Assessing 'Suitability' with Regard to 'Institutions'
137. An assessment of 'suitability' may be carried out from two standpoints. One, on a general level, involves evaluating the extent to which facilities meet certain basic criteria. The other, with a more 'micro' focus, is to determine how appropriately a given facility responds to the specific needs of the children in its care.

138. Seeking guidance from the CRC itself as regards basic conditions to be respected, it is necessary to turn to Article 3(3), where these are set out in a somewhat minimalist manner: 'institutions, services and facilities for the care or protection of children shall conform with the standards established by competent authorities, particularly in the area of safety, health, in the number and suitability of their staff, as well as competent supervision'. Standard-setting in these regards is therefore left entirely to the authorities of each State Party – though implicitly and necessarily in conformity with other obligations contained elsewhere in the CRC.

---

[138] See for example I. Sinclair, K. Wilson and I. Gibbs, *Foster placements: why they succeed and why they fail* (London/Philadelphia, Jessica Kingsley Publishers, 2004).

139. This aspect of suitability will thus involve determining how well residential facilities protect and promote the whole range of civil, economic, social and cultural rights to be enjoyed by children. There is no indication in the CRC of any basic requirements regarding, for example, the size, location, regime or ultimate goal of a facility that would condition, in part at least, its ability to fulfil those tasks. It is necessary to look to subsequent texts for inspiration in that regard.

140. One such text is the above-mentioned Council of Europe Recommendation,[139] which not only recalls the principal rights of children that are to be upheld during care but also lists elements of 'basic principles' and 'guidelines and quality standards' for care facilities. These include:

- the child's successful social integration or re-integration should be the primary objective of a placement;
- any measures of control or discipline should be based on public regulations and approved standards;
- placement as close as possible to the child's environment and organized to allow parents to exercise their responsibilities and to maintain parent-child contact on a regular basis;
- a small family-style living unit should be provided;
- an individual care plan should be drawn up;
- internal organization based on the quality and stability of living units, high professional standards of the staff, adequate salaries, stability of staff, multi-disciplinary teamwork, effective child-centred use of available resources, and means and specific training to develop appropriate cooperation with the child's parents.

141. In addition, many children in residential care are the subject of 'placement orders' or the equivalent, and will hence be covered by the 1990 UN Rules for the Protection of Juveniles Deprived of their Liberty. Although these Rules were primarily developed in relation to juvenile offenders, their scope explicitly includes 'placement of a person [under the age of 18] in a public or private custodial setting, from which this person is not permitted to leave at will, by order of any judicial, administrative or other public authority.' Hence the Rules apply 'also to [juveniles] deprived of liberty in health and welfare placements [. . .] They are elaborations of the basic

---

[139] Council of Europe, Rec (2005)5 (*cf. supra* note 66).

principles found in the Convention on the Rights of the Child.'[140] Among the most pertinent provisions concerning children placed in care facilities from which they may not leave at will are those specifying standards in relation to:

- Record-keeping (IV.A)
- Interviews upon admission, and the preparation of a psychological and social report identifying factors that help to determine the type and level of care required (IV.C)
- Physical environment and accommodation, including right to privacy (IV.D)
- Education and vocational training (IV.E)
- Recreation (IV.F)
- Religion (IV.G)
- Medical care (IV.H)
- Contacts with the wider community (IV.J)
- Limitations of physical restraint and the use of force (IV.K)
- Disciplinary procedures (IV.L)
- Inspection and complaints (IV.M)
- Return to the community (IV.N)
- Personnel (V).

142. The Implementation Handbook for the Convention on the Rights of the Child also lists a number of requirements that would indicate the suitability of institutions in its 'Implementation Checklist' given at the end of each section.[141] Here, the criteria that institutions have to fulfil are understood in broader terms, *e.g.* that they should 'respect children's human dignity, provide children with as normal a life as possible and take all measures to secure their integration in society'. Over and above that, institutions should ascertain the views of the child and secure children's rights under the Convention.[142]

143. The other side of the 'suitability' coin is that the facility meets, in a positive manner, the needs of the individual child concerned at a given moment in time, with that child's future in mind. This aspect of suitability

---

[140] G. van Bueren, *International Standards concerning the Rights of the Child No. 3: Introduction to United Nations Rules for the Protection of Juveniles Deprived of their Liberty* (Geneva, Defence for Children International, 1995).

[141] Section on Article 20, 'Children deprived of their family environment', in R. Hodgkin and P. Newell, *o.c.* (note 27).

[142] *Ibid.*, pp. 266–267.

thus not only depends on the validity of the decision-making process regarding the placement of a given child – including an effective 'gate-keeping' system – and the availability of a full range of placement options in practice, but is also inextricably linked to the obligation to ensure 'periodic review' of any placement for the purpose of care and protection (Article 25). Equally it calls into play the proper application of the child's right to have his or her best interests underlie all decisions (Article 3) and to have his or her views thereon taken into account (Article 12).

144. It follows that one criterion for determining a facility's 'suitability' is the extent to which it works, within the child care system, to ensure that a child remains there only as long as is necessary. This means that it should both initiate and cooperate with efforts to secure, wherever possible, the child's return to the family under appropriate conditions – in keeping with Article 7 – or his or her move to another 'permanent' family-based setting as suggested by the reference in the preamble to the desirability of a 'family environment' for a child. A major problem associated with 'institutional placements' is that in practice they too often become long-term or permanent precisely because effective responsibilities are not assigned for identifying appropriate alternatives for each child as the placement proceeds and his or her situation evolves.

3.7   'Continuity in Upbringing' and 'Ethnic, Religious, Cultural and Linguistic Background'

145. Consideration of the general question – dealt with in the final sentence of paragraph 3 of Article 20 of the CRC – of preventing undue disruption in the life of a child in alternative care was ostensibly instigated by a proposal submitted to the Working Group in 1985 by the Four Directions Council, a body representing certain indigenous peoples in North America. Advocating respect for the equality of all cultures, it submitted the following additional draft text:

> 'No separation of the child from his parents or community, or alternative family care, shall have as its objective or effect the denial of the child's right to have, learn or adopt the culture of his parents.'[143]

146. The basic concern of the Four Directions Council was clearly to oppose the practice, current or known in a number of countries, of removing children

---

[143] Proposal by the Four Directions Council submitted to the Working Group in 1985 (UN Doc. E/CN.4/1985/WG.1/NGO.1, 1985), p. 2.

of indigenous origin from the care of their parents because of alleged abuse or neglect and deliberately placing them with non-indigenous foster or adoptive families.[144] This submission prompted others, by governments, that were to develop and broaden considerably the issue at hand, to such an extent that it is unclear how far the original concern still underpinned the text finally adopted – the *Travaux Préparatoires* shed little or no light on this. The new proposals dealt with the two distinct – though clearly connected – elements of 'continuity' and ethno-cultural considerations.

147. The concept of 'continuity in upbringing' used in Article 20 has no precedent in international instruments, although it was subsequently incorporated *verbatim* into the African Charter.[145] It was first mentioned in a written proposal to the Working Group[146] that was adopted without either its precise intended meaning or its implications being broached during the initial debate on the question (1987) or at any subsequent stage of the drafting. In particular, there is therefore no indication as to if and how 'continuity in a child's upbringing' is intended to relate to 'the right to continuing care', as set out in the 1986 Declaration (Article 5), or to the concept of 'continuity of care', or how it might relate to 'care . . . by continuous care-givers', the term subsequently used in the UNHCR Guidelines on Refugee Children, mentioned previously.

148. While reference to the overall issue of 'ethno-cultural' considerations also has its origins in the above-mentioned Four Directions Council proposal, the final wording was inspired by Article 27 of the CCPR. The word 'cultural' was added following the Technical Review stage to take account of the right of minority groups to 'enjoy their own culture' (stipulated in Article 27 of the CCPR as well as in Article 30 of the CRC), 'the right of everyone . . . to take part in cultural life' (Article 15 of the CESCR), as well as Article 24 of the 1986 Declaration – although here it relates solely to international adoption – whereby 'due regard shall be given to the child's cultural and religious background'. The final formulation indeed largely mirrors the scope of Article 30 of the CRC, which deals with the rights of children belonging to 'ethnic, religious or linguistic minorities' or who are 'indigenous'

---

[144] See for example Australian Human Rights & Equal Opportunity Commission, *Bringing them home*, A National Inquiry into the Separation of Aboriginal and Torres Strait Islander Children from their Families (Commonwealth of Australia, HREOC, 1997).

[145] Article XXV(3).

[146] A proposal to the 1987 Working Group by the Netherlands and the United Kingdom (UN Doc. E/CN.4/1987/WG.1/WP.24, 1987).

to enjoy their own culture, to profess and practice their own religion and to use their own language.

149. In examining the substance of this provision, it is first necessary to re-emphasize that, while connected, the questions of 'continuity' and 'background' should not be seen as one and the same issue. The text of Article 20 does not explicitly demand 'continuity . . . in the child's . . . background' but requires that due regard be paid both *to* continuity in upbringing and *to* the child's background.

150. It would therefore be questionable to state, for instance, that according to the CRC, '[i]n making such [care] arrangements, due regard has to be given to continuity in the child's upbringing *in terms of* his/her religious, ethnic, cultural and linguistic background'[147] [our emphasis]. Other facets of 'upbringing' – including stable relationships, for example – also need to be taken into account for continuity: '[p]aramount in the lives of children and young persons is their need for continuity with their primary attachment figures.'[148]

151. The lack of clarity, noted above, as to the intended meaning of 'continuity in upbringing' poses problems. The term 'upbringing' is more especially associated with the role of the parents or other primary caregivers in ensuring a child's development and well-being.[149] On that basis, when others necessarily take over that primary care-giving role as foreseen in Article 20, the aim of 'continuity in upbringing' might logically be inferred as promoting constancy of the substitute caregiver and, in particular, avoidance of destabilizing 'serial placements'.[150] At the same time, given both the immediate context of the term and the CRC's recognition of other influences on child development,[151] 'continuity in a child's upbringing' might

---

[147] WHO South East Asia Region, *Towards a Better Tomorrow: Child Rights and Health*, undated, available at http://w3.whosea.org/crc/coverf.htm

[148] New South Wales Office of the Children's Guardian, *Accreditation Benchmark Policy Statement*, Casework to Support Permanency, Benchmark Policy 1.4, 2003.

[149] Thus, for example, Article 18(1) of the CRC: 'Parents or, as the case may be, legal guardians, have the primary responsibility for the upbringing and development of the child.'

[150] For a good discussion of the principle of 'continuity in upbringing' with regard to the situation of unaccompanied refugee children see D.J. Steinbock, 'Unaccompanied Refugee Children in Host Country Foster Families', *International Journal of Refugee Law* 8, No. 1/2, 1996, pp. 6–48.

[151] Thus, Article 29 of the CRC stipulates the *aims of education* as including 'the development of respect for [. . .] his or her own cultural identity, language and values' and 'the preparation of the child for responsible life in a free society, in the spirit of understanding, peace, tolerance, equality of sexes, and friendship among all peoples, ethnic, national and

equally validly be taken to imply maintaining the child not only in a stable care setting, but also in the same socio-cultural environment – and even in the same educational setting.

152. Certainly, when the importance of continuity for a child's harmonious development is considered, it is invariably broached in wider terms than that related solely to the caregiver and is usually linked to socio-cultural aspects. Thus, New Zealand's Children, Young Persons and their Families Act (1989) states that, when children cannot return to their own family, 'they should be placed in a family setting that allows for continuity of the child's individual and cultural identity.'[152] In the same vein, '[t]he value of and the need for continuity in a child's ethnic or cultural background has now been widely acknowledged and accepted'[153] and '[c]ulture provides children with identity and continuity.'[154]

153. This combination of 'continuity' and 'background' in Article 20 has also been frequently employed to support the use of kinship care as opposed to other in-country alternative care solutions: 'these criteria are more likely to be met by an extended family member than by placement with foster parents or a government agency.'[155] Similarly, 'keeping children within their own kinship, community, and cultural networks – the concept of continuity – has found international favour in contemporary child welfare practice'[156] and 'kinship care [. . .] allows the child to stay in a familiar environment and thus provides some level of continuity in his/her social and affective development.'[157]

---

religious groups and persons of indigenous origin', corresponding largely to the consideration in the CRC Preamble that 'the child should be fully prepared to live an individual life in society and *brought up* in [. . .] the spirit of peace, dignity, tolerance, freedom, equality and solidarity'. [our emphasis]

[152] P. Boshier, *Care and Protection of Children: New Zealand and Australian Experience of Cross-Border Co-operation* (paper presented at the 4th World Congress on Family Law and Children's Rights, Cape Town, South Africa, 20–23 March 2005).

[153] C. Bojorge, 'Intercountry Adoptions: In the Best Interests of the Child?', *QUT Law and Justice Journal* 15, No. 2002, electronic journal, pages not specified, at: http://bar.austlii.edu.au/au/journals/QUTLJJ/2002/15.html.

[154] UNICEF, *Reference Guide on Protecting the Rights of Child Victims of Trafficking in Europe*, UNICEF Regional Office for CEE/CIS, 2006.

[155] S. Ruxton, *Separated children and EU asylum and immigration policy* (Copenhagen, Save the Children Denmark, 2003).

[156] J. Worrall, 'Kinship care of the abused child: the New Zealand experience', *Child Welfare* 80, No. 5, 2001, pp. 497–511.

[157] ISS, *A Global Policy for the Protection of Children Deprived of Parental Care*, submission to the CRC General Day of Discussion, 16 September 2006.

154. Indeed, the potential implications of this provision when viewed in this way are considerable. The PACE is not alone in having cited it in order, for example, to advocate against recourse to intercountry adoption: '[t]he present tendencies of international adoption go against [Article 20 of] the UN Convention on the Rights of the Child'.[158]

155. This said, it is clear from the text of Article 20 that there is no absolute duty to ensure continuity or to base alternative care decisions on the child's background, but only to have 'due regard' for each of these factors. With respect to the implications of this provision for policy and practice, an appreciation of what constitutes 'due regard' is necessarily to be founded more especially on an assessment of the best interests of the child in each case, as well as on the CRC's other general principles of non-discrimination, right to survival and development and right to be heard.

156. In terms of the level and nature of the obligation created by this provision, it can also be noted that, while the English text refers to 'the desirability of continuity', the French version stipulates 'the necessity of a certain continuity' [our translation]. These renderings would seem to have somewhat different implications. Having due regard to 'desirability' is less forceful than to 'necessity', whereas 'continuity' alone is clearly more absolute than 'a certain continuity'. As far as can be determined, the ramifications of these conflicting approaches have so far not been examined.

4. A Tentative Summary

157. This Commentary raises a wide range of issues regarding the implications of the scope and substantive rights set out in Article 20, and the results of discussion thereof cannot always be conclusive. Nonetheless, it seems possible to make a number of general observations on key points in a very summary form, by way of conclusion.

158. State obligations under this provision are towards any child within their jurisdiction who, for whatever reason, is unable to benefit, or has been removed, from the care of his or her parents and is not being looked after informally within the extended family. The notable exception in principle is a child who, alleged or convicted of being in conflict with the law, is

---

[158] Parliamentary Assembly of the Council of Europe, *Recommendation on International Adoption: Respecting Children's Rights*, Rec 1443 (2000), 26 January 2000.

deprived of his or her family environment in direct consequence. While the wider community's potential role in providing care is recognized, the community cannot necessarily be assimilated with a child's family environment, so a State's obligations under this article towards a child cared for in the community remain untouched. The exact nature of the obligations to provide special protection and assistance remains unclear, however, with regard to children in certain situations, including in particular those in child-headed households or living in the street.

159. When fulfilling its obligation to ensure alternative care for a child, the State has to consider which of a range of options corresponds best to the situation and the short- and longer-term needs of each child. It is to undertake its assessment by reviewing in turn the potential suitability of placement within the extended family, in a family-based foster setting (including *kafala*) or as a last resort in a residential facility, with the ultimate aim of securing the child's return to his or her family environment or his or her adoption wherever possible. At the same time, every effort should be made to identify a suitable option that causes the least possible disruption to the child's life, enabling him or her to remain as far as possible within the same socio-cultural context and avoiding serial placements. While it is desirable to seek and develop non-institutional responses in general to children requiring alternative care, their use must be deemed both appropriate and effective in meeting the needs of the child in question. The necessity and suitability of whichever of these placements is decided – including formal kinship care – must be monitored and regularly reviewed, in consultation with the child and his or her family.

160. The State is responsible for ensuring the well-being and protection of a child in whatever alternative care setting he or she is placed, implying a robust authorization, monitoring and inspection activity based on agreed criteria and standards. However, in the case of informal – *i.e.* not ordered by an administrative or judicial authority – care within the extended family, the State's welfare and protection obligations towards the child are analogous to those towards a child living in the parental home. This in principle implies that the State is made aware of such informal arrangements, but it is then neither required nor encouraged to authorize or monitor them in any way that goes beyond its general child protection obligations.

161. Our Commentary demonstrates that there are still numerous lacunae in national, regional and, particularly, international legislation as concerns the effective safeguarding of the rights of children living outside their family

environment. Policies targeting the well-being of children without a family and aiming to secure these children's rights seem to be characterized by frequent inconsistencies and 'grey zones', notably with regard to a) what counts as a family environment, and consequently, what counts as *deprivation* of a family environment and b) by what standards an alternative family environment should be measured. Enhancing the homogeneity of national legislations and policy approaches thus appears to be the first step to guaranteeing that the children concerned experience minimal disruption in their lives and that they ultimately find themselves in a stable and harmonious environment that promotes their personal, emotional and physical development to the fullest possible extent.

REFERENCES

American Academy of Pediatrics, 'Health Care for Children and Adolescents in the Juvenile Correctional Care System', *Pediatrics* 107, No. 4, 2001, 799–803.

Blackstock, C. and Alderman, J.A., 'The State and Aboriginal children in the child welfare system in Canada', *Early Childhood Matters*, No. 105, 2005, 19–22.

Bojorge, C., 'Intercountry Adoptions: In the Best Interests of the Child?' *QUT Law and Justice Journal* 15, 2002, electronic journal, no pages specified, available at: http://bar.austlii.edu.au/au/journals/QUTLJJ/2002/15.html.

Boshier, P., 'Care and Protection of Children: New Zealand and Australian Experience of Cross-Border Co-operation', paper presented at 4th World Congress on Family Law and Children's Rights, Cape Town, South Africa, 20–23 March 2005.

Courtney, M. E., Roderick, M., Smithgall, C., Gladden, R.M. and Nagaoka, J., 'The Educational Status of Foster Children', *Chapin Hall Center for Children Issue Brief*, No. 102, 2004, 1–6.

Detrick, S. (ed.), *The United Nations Convention on the Rights of the Child. A Guide to the Travaux Préparatoires*, Dordrecht: Martinus Nijhoff Publishers, 1992.

Doherty, G., *The Long-Term Effects of Non-Parental Child Care*, Toronto: University of Toronto, 1996.

Dumitriu-Segnana, E., *Case Law of the European Court of Human Rights related to child rights, role of the families and alternative care*, paper presented at International Conference on Child Rights, Bucharest, Romania, 2–3 February 2006.

Foster, G., 'The capacity of the extended family safety net for orphans in Africa', *Psychology, Health & Medicine* 5, No. 1, 2000, 55–62.

Hall, M., 'The Liability of Public Authorities for the Abuse of Children in Institutional Care: Common Law Developments in Canada and the United Kingdom', *International Journal of Law, Policy and the Family* 14, No. 3, 2000, 281–301.

Hodgkin, R. and Newell, P., *Implementation Handbook for the Convention on the Rights of the Child*, New York: UNICEF, 2002.

Kilkelly, U., 'The Best of Both Worlds for Children's Rights? Interpreting the European Convention on Human Rights in the Light of the UN Convention on the Rights of the Child', *Human Rights Quarterly* 23, No. 2, 2001, 308–326.

Kilkelly, U., *The Child and the European Convention on Human Rights*, Aldershot: Ashgate, 1999.

MacLellan, M., 'Child Headed Households: Dilemmas of Definition and Livelihood Rights', paper presented at 4th World Congress on Family Law and Children's Rights, Cape Town, South Africa, March 2005.

Maxwell, D., 'An Asset Account for Looked After Children; A proposal to improve education outcomes for children in care', London: Institute for Public Policy Research, 2006.

Milligan, I., Hunter, L. and Kendrick, A., *Current trends in the use of residential child care in Scotland*, Glasgow: Scottish Institute of Residential Child Care, 2006.

Monasch, R. and Boerma, T.J., 'Orphanhood and childcare patterns in sub-Saharan Africa: an analysis of national surveys from 40 countries', *AIDS* 18, No. suppl. 1, 2004, 55–65.

Rosa, S., *Counting on Children. Realising the right to social assistance for child-headed households in South Africa*, Cape Town: University of Cape Town, 2004.

Ruxton, S., *Separated children and EU asylum and immigration policy*, Copenhagen: Save the Children Denmark, 2003.

Sinclair, I., Wilson, K. and Gibbs, I., *Foster placements: why the succeed and why they fail*, London/Philadelphia: Jessica Kingsley Publishers, 2004.

Steinbock, D.J., 'Unaccompanied Refugee Children in Host Country Foster Families', *International Journal of Refugee Law* 8, No. 1/2, 1996, pp. 6–48.

UNHCR, *UNHCR Guidelines on the Formal Determination of the Best Interests of the Child*, Geneva: UNHCR, 2006.

UNICEF, *Child Protection and Children Affected by AIDS: A Companion Paper to the Framework for the Protection, Care and Support of Orphans and Vulnerable Children Living in a World with HIV and AIDS*, New York: UNICEF, 2006.

UNICEF Innocenti Research Centre, *Children and Disability in Transition in CEE/CIS and Baltic States*, Florence: UNICEF, 2005.

van Bueren, G., 'Combating Child Poverty – Human Rights Approaches', *Human Rights Quarterly* 21, No. 3, 1999, 680–706.

—— (ed.), *International Documents on Children*, Dordrecht: Martinus Nijhoff Publishers, 1993.

Worrall, J., 'Kinship care of the abused child: the New Zealand experience', *Child Welfare* 80, No. 5, 2001, 497–511.